HEALING INTELLIGENCE

HEALING INTELLIGENCE
The Spirit in Psychotherapy
Working with Darkness
and Light

Alan Mulhern

KARNAC

First published in 2012 by
Karnac Books Ltd
118 Finchley Road
London NW3 5HT

British Library Cataloguing in Publication Data

A C.I.P. for this book is available from the British Library

ISBN-13: 978-1-78049-039-7

Typeset by Vikatan Publishing Solutions (P) Ltd., Chennai, India

Printed in Great Britain

www.karnacbooks.com

CONTENTS

ACKNOWLEDGEMENTS

I am grateful to the Jungians of the Asociación Venezolana de Psicología Analítica, especially to Luis Sanz and Gonzalo Himiob, for their enthusiastic reception of a 2005 talk of mine, *The Spirit in Psychotherapy*, in Caracas, Venezuela—invaluable fuel for the journey to come; similarly, to the Association of Jungian Analysts, London, where I trained, which also received a talk on this theme in 2006 and gave warm support.

I wish to thank Nadya Berlin who communicated the wisdom of the Sufi path and the intuition of the heart; warm thanks to colleagues who gave me valuable help: Mark Dunn, for insightful feedback and directing me to my inner muse; Lindsey Harris who gave appreciation of the text, also providing, most generously, all the illustrations for the book; Anne Young, who supplied detailed comments on early chapters; Dale Mathers, who corrected an early draft and gave a sense of what was in front of me; Jack Bierschenk, who carefully corrected a first manuscript; Gill Stuart, who gave feedback and personal insight; a special thanks to Susan Taylor who gave many hours of work, providing inspiring feedback on a late draft alongside minute and even poetic editorial scrutiny.

Warm thanks to Martin Stone, my training analyst, who helped restore a wounded soul and taught me the alignment to the deep psyche; also to Rogan Taylor, who first introduced me, inspirationally, to the works of Jung and the unity of East and West.

Deep gratitude to Melanie Mulhern, my daughter, who unreservedly supported this project throughout, a wonderful *aide de camp*, who listened to many a tale of the fatigued and sometimes manic author, corrected manuscripts, "talked the talk" of the "real" world, and helped in a multitude of practical matters. Deep thanks to Diamora, my wife, who provided loving support during the time of preparation and writing, who listened most patiently to the vicissitudes of the journey from when it was only a twinkle in the eye; also for her communications on the work of healing in the Craniosacral Therapy field, providing comparison with another discipline in which she qualified during the time of writing.

I am most grateful to my clients who have time and again taught me, by their dedication and courage, the ways of the deep psyche. All case studies here are composite creations and none refer directly to any individual, whose identities have been carefully disguised.

Last, and not least, I give acknowledgement to my inner muse, Aceso, the Greek goddess of healing, whose gentle guidance and deep support made this journey not only possible but joyful.

* * *

Notes on the illustrations

The front cover and other illustrations were designed and produced especially for the book by Lindsey Harris, a Jungian analyst and visual artist with a special interest in the creative potential of the psyche and the power of the imagination to bring about inner healing. She possesses an understanding of mythological and alchemical imagery as a metaphor of the psychological path of individuation. The various symbols, themes and motifs of the artwork were developed as visual metaphors for the contents of the chapters and were conceived, altered, and refined in collaborative communication with myself. Lindsey has a private practice in England.

The front cover has as its symbol the serpent and pearl, central to the book, and interpreted in Chapter Six's rendering of the Hymn of the Pearl. Its source of inspiration is the Shiva Bindu, mentioned at least twice in Jung's collected works. In volume 4 Jung comments:

The serpentine line leading to the vessel is analogous to the healing serpent of Aesculapius and also to the tantric symbol of Shiva Bindu, the creative latent God, without extension in space, who in the form of a point or lingam is encircled three and a half times by the Kundalini serpent.

(*CW*, Vol. 4)

In Volume 9a, with reference to the symbol of a serpent coiling around a circular object, Jung further elaborates:

... the divine power before creation, the opposites are still united. The god rests in the point. Hence the snake signifies extension, the mother of becoming, the creation of the world of forms. In India this point is called the Hiranyagarbha, "golden germ" or "golden egg" ... We read in the *Sanatsugatiya* "That pure great light which is radiant, that great glory which the gods worship, which makes the sun shine forth, that divine eternal being is perceived by the faithful".

(*CW*, Vol. 9a, p. 368, p. 414)

Among the many interpretations of this powerful symbol the Shiva Bindu can be conceived as an antinomy, a unity of opposites—the great still point and the encircling energies of creation held in balance. In this book it is, therefore, valued as a symbol of integration.

The introduction shows a staff of Asclepius, a traditional symbol of medicine and healing; Chapter One shows the Pilgrim and the Mount; Chapter Two an alignment motif; Chapter Three refers to the well known illustrations of the alchemical Rosarium Philosophorum (*CW*, Vol. 16); Chapter Four illustrates the tale of Percival, the Grail, and the Fisher King—a metaphor of the spiritual search but also exploring the integration symbols of the journey; Chapter Six shows a mandala, created using sacred geometry, symbolising healing intelligence centred in the self; Chapter Seven ends, playfully, with a ship/lighthouse (question/reflection) image presided over by the Sol and Luna of alchemical fame.

Alan Mulhern, a Jungian psychotherapist, has worked for twenty-five years in private practice in London. He has given numerous workshops in both the UK and in Venezuela on subjects such as dream analysis, narcissism, the shadow, psychoanalytic diagnosis, and healing in psychotherapy. He has written on the subject of the changes in the profession of psychotherapy in the modern age.

PREFACE

The origin of this book lay in a conference, some years ago, in which notable Jungian psychotherapists were giving an overview of the principles guiding their practice. The question of what is healing in psychotherapy did not arise, so I asked how they believed healing worked. None were inclined to reply until one remarked: "That is the $64000 question and if I had the answer to it I would retire to the hills of Hollywood." General laughter followed. Clearly, healing was not on the agenda for serious analysts. Individuation, yes, but healing, well ... not quite. This was a more "alternative" topic, associated with celebrities, perhaps charlatanism, image rather than substance. It was certainly mysterious. The matter, however, remained not just as a personal struggle but increasingly, in my view, a crucial issue in psychotherapy. This book has emerged as a result of that unanswered question.

While Freudian psychoanalysis was a foundation for much of my analytic work, it was the field opened up by Jung that provided a connection to the transformative aspects of the psyche, especially of psychological growth in adulthood. From this viewpoint there was an inner directing centre, a guidance system that could be found in the unconscious, capable of redirecting and developing personality. Jung was to explore some extraordinary metaphors for this process, such as alchemy, conscious that the thing in itself, healing intelligence, needed to be studied as a symbol, in its manifestation, since its direct apprehension was not possible. Jung's main focus was on his concept of individuation, the healing intentionality of the whole personality, especially in the second half of life. However, there are many healing moments on this larger journey and various emotional wounds from which one may suffer. The question of how healing works became more intriguing as I puzzled upon it. It is customary in psychotherapy to ask clients why they feel bad. However, I now began to question why they felt better and attempted to decipher the dynamics of this healing. While a great deal had been written on the big picture of individuation very little had been written on the more microscopic subject of how healing occurs within the psyche as a discrete event.

In my early practice I was reasonably skilled at exploring the negativity and darkness in the psyche, having spent years investigating plenty of my own. Thus, I had a lot of experience in learning to share my problems, of catharsis, of listening to my deeper psyche and gradually reshaping my life more in line with its guidance. Such is the path of many who undertake a serious journey in psychotherapy. However, it was much longer before I could work with the light in the psyche (in fact it was probably a long time before I even learnt to lighten up) and to realize that darkness and light have to be worked with together to facilitate a healing outcome. Thus, I learnt to value the healing intelligence that can manifest as light in the inner world, to cherish and enjoy the light of inner awareness, to recognise the potency of healing energy, to listen, evoke, cooperate and work with it, to appreciate the higher powers of illuminative intuition and even transcendental love. Very slowly I learnt to work with the light, finding it every bit as important as working with darkness, in fact experiencing them as an interconnected energy field. This increased my respect for the numinous force and power of healing intelligence. In particular, I wished to describe it more closely, to work with it more effectively.

The more that therapists have experienced the transformative field in their own psyche the more they are inclined to help others, finding meaning and even joy at so doing. I was fortunate in my personal psychotherapy to become more conscious of my darkness, negativity, distortions, and defences so I could go some way towards healing my wounds. There are no methods described in this book I have not tried many times on myself. All have been tried by others before me, by one means or another, in psychotherapy, spiritual groups, alternative healing practices, and in some cases for thousands of years in the East, and found to be of value. They are not simply theoretical but are based on experience and practice, and have proved to be effective. At key points I have made references to other psychotherapists (such as Jung, Assagioli, Welwood, and Vaughan, to name a few), whose work is concerned with precisely the same area, who have developed concrete, communicable ways of helping clients and have struggled to articulate this mysterious process in a language others can understand. This book, too, attempts to describe the subtle yet powerful healing intelligence that permeates the psyche.

Even in the Jungian community this concept of healing is not easy to talk about meaningfully. Many psychotherapists know it exists, have experienced it both personally and with their clients. Yet it is hard to describe. It is rarely on the syllabi of training institutes. Frances Vaughan wrote:

> The idea of healing the whole person is not new, but accessing inner healing for the psyche is an art in which few practitioners are truly skilled … Traditionally trained clinicians were found to be completely unprepared to deal with spiritual concerns, although they were frequently called upon to do so.
>
> (Vaughan, 1986)

With the expansion of psychotherapy and counselling such knowledge is becoming even rarer. Many training programmes are lighter in their requirements for personal therapy and there is greater demand for shorter, evidence based practice—hardly the conditions to explore the enigmatic concept of healing intelligence.

Certainly there is something about healing intelligence that is inherently paradoxical. On the one hand, to the awakened eye, it appears everywhere, not only universally in the human psyche but also in the body, in the animal kingdom, in life itself. On the other hand, trying to grasp it is like water that slips through one's hand—there is something naturally esoteric and elusive about it. It does not matter how this concept is laid out; it cannot be appreciated except by those who have suffered and consciously transformed themselves; nobody can work with it unless they have experienced it in their own psyche.

The truism that one can only promote healing in another to the extent one has healed oneself is half the story—a very important half admittedly. However, even after some degree of personal healing, its dynamics may remain mostly unconscious. I needed to work for many years as a practitioner before I could begin to express in words a little of its mystery. Even when my ideas became clearer and my work more effective, it was a great challenge to articulate it more coherently. One needs therefore not only to experience but to practice and struggle with it.

I am content therefore to address this book to a specific audience—not just those who want to know of healing but those who need to. First, I direct it to those who, regardless of profession, wish not only to know more of the dynamics of the psyche but also feel compelled to heal their wounds. It is also intended for trainees in psychotherapy and counselling who must explore their psyche more deeply. Beyond these, particular members of spiritual groups, churches, and religions, interested by the interface of psychotherapy and spirituality, will hopefully find in this book much to interest them. There are also many clients in psychotherapy and counselling deeply attracted to these questions of healing and spirituality in their personal journey. Others, working in healing disciplines, complementary or alternative to psychotherapy, may also be intensely concerned with matters of healing. Knowledge of how healing works should be an interdisciplinary affair and much can be learnt from those in other fields. But above all I address it to fellow practitioners, particularly those who are called upon to work actively with spiritual matters in psychotherapy. These include analysts, psychotherapists, and counsellors of Jungian, Existential, Humanist, Integrative, Transpersonal, and other persuasions who are intrigued and compelled by the question of how healing intelligence works in the psyche.

What is healing?

Healing energies are a natural intelligence within the psyche, promoting the unconscious state of wholeness we call health. This health is, for the most part, intensely desired by those who suffer pain, division, and conflict within themselves; for some it is the central goal of life to recover it.

Emotional wounds come in many forms: damage to one's sense of self; painful or crippling experiences of loss, deprivation, trauma, abuse; love wounds of rejection and betrayal. These can clearly cause not just pain but also limit the capacity to function or grow. The psyche can also be distorted, incomplete, in conflict with itself, or can repress vital areas of its own functioning. In addition, there may be spiritual wounds such as anguish suffered by those who feel incomplete or at odds with their culture. Typically, the dreams of such people speak of a sense of damage or alienation. Clearly, the range and intensity of emotional wounding is considerable.

Emotional healing may be sought from many sources, the most common being from another person. The child turns to the mother, the adult to a friend, the lover to her partner. In each case the receiving of some comfort, or preferably love, is the great healer, allowing one to feel whole. Another source is religion; again it is often the input of love, in this case divine, which seems to flow from the outer to the inner world, bringing healing and an experience of wholeness. Spiritual healing may channel energy as if from a transcendent and universal source to the wounded. In some religious movements a guru may be a source of wisdom and love thus promoting feelings of wholeness in the disciple. In the Christian religion love has been exalted as its supreme value. Paul in his famous letter to the Corinthians writes:

> If I speak with the tongues of men, and of angels, and have not love, I am become as sounding brass ... And if I should have prophecy and should know all mysteries, and all knowledge, and if I should have all faith, so that I could remove mountains, and have not love, I am nothing ... And now these three remain: faith, hope and love. But the greatest of these is love.
>
> (I Corinthians 13:1–13)

Music, architecture, art, dance, or literature can move the deepest areas of the psyche, express its highest sentiments, connect the individual to the universal and promote a sense of wholeness. The experience of nature may also be a source of healing. For the poet Wordsworth there was a numinous, natural intelligence, and love permeating all nature and the soul of man:

> A presence ... Whose dwelling is the light of setting suns ...
> A motion and a spirit that impels
> All thinking things, all objects of all thought,
> And rolls through all things.

> (Wordsworth, *Tintern Abbey*, 93–102)

Spiritual energies, at first perceived on the outside, connect man to his deeper psyche in which transcendent and healing forces are found inside the psyche.

In many of the sources mentioned above the inner sense of wholeness is dependent on something or someone outside of oneself. If the outside source is taken away serious results may follow, such as depression or even psychosis. However, not everyone can find healing outside of themselves. Loved ones may not be available, some people remain alone, some are betrayed or disappointed in love, others do not have strong families to contain their identity. Many people in the modern world can no longer turn to a personal God. In these cases they may be obliged by personal suffering to look for the source of healing within themselves, which frequently requires a mobilisation and focus of extra-ordinary energy upon emotional and spiritual distress. To find this source within oneself, without help, is possible but can be painfully difficult and confusing. Therefore it often takes place in a dual relationship of the healer and the wounded. There is a special quality when a practitioner helps to mobilise, focus, and augment this natural healing energy within the sufferer.

In physical medicine one can list the various types of wounds and their stages of healing such as the inflammatory, proliferative, and remodelling phases. Healing can be regenerative or a repairing type of operation. Physical healing, however, is as mysterious as emotional healing. Deepak Chopra says:

> When your body mends a broken bone why is that not a miracle?
> As a healing process it is certainly complex, far too complex for

medicine to duplicate; it involves an incredible number of perfectly synchronised processes, of which medicine knows only the major ones and those imperfectly.

(Chopra, 1989, p. 16)

However, although physical healing is an extremely powerful and complex process it does not always happen cleanly but can be blocked, interrupted, or fail, leading to chronic wounds that won't heal. Infections, old age, diabetes, or arterial disease may contribute to this. Even a brief glance at the role of healing in biological processes leads to useful comparisons when one ponders the role of healing in psychological conditions. It is clear that, like physical healing in the body, there are different forms of emotional healing; some are profound, others more superficial. Healing, while being largely instinctual in the body, can easily be blocked or prevented from functioning in the psyche by repressive mechanisms. Trauma may overwhelm natural healing functions. Just as healing intelligence has many sources in the body, so too are there multiple sources in the psyche for dealing with wounds and traumas.

At its most natural, healing in the psyche is an unconscious issue. It can happen outside of our awareness much as physical damage tends to heal itself. Many emotional wounds, such as the loss of a loved one or damage to one's self esteem, tend to heal or partially heal with the passage of time. This is not the subject of reason or under the control of the ego. However, this natural process of healing can be blocked in the psyche as it can in the body. It is the task of practitioners to help find ways of releasing it, to provide the right environment for it to express itself, to stimulate its action and contribute their own healing energy. Blocked healing, sometimes the result of deep emotional damage or rigid forms of upbringing that distort character development, requires extra-special efforts. Repair is not taking place automatically here. In these cases healing in the psyche is an extra-normal journey requiring access to the transformative energies of the psyche.

This book condenses my experience of healing in one discipline, Jungian psychotherapy. It will have many cross-over points where those in other schools besides Jungian, as well as other disciplines besides psychotherapy, will recognise much of what is being said. The word "healing" would not be acceptable to many psychotherapists as a description of what they do. Significant sections of the psychotherapy profession have become more rational in their methodology and less inclined even towards any idea of the unconscious. Instead, the fascination with healing energy has flooded into alternative therapies which abound in the Western world. This book explores an elusive concept, healing intelligence, which, in my view, is nevertheless at the core of depth psychotherapy. It easily becomes lost under the weight of formal government requirements, health agencies, the ever-increasing demands for transparency and accountability in the profession. It is readily dismissed as ephemeral, immeasurable, and of no consequence; yet things of most value may have least worth in the eyes of the world. Dreams and the contents of our inner world give us ample evidence of the importance of listening to the intelligence lying in the psyche, aligning ourselves to this wisdom, and connecting to its healing, transformative powers.

Healing intelligence can be activated and stimulated by a special form of awareness—here simply called *inner awareness*—and expresses itself via symbols. Psychotherapists with knowledge of healing may be skilled in encouraging and mobilising this special awareness and healing energy within the sufferer. Based on their own experience of suffering they have undergone the transformative, archetypal journeys towards wholeness. The method of their own personal healing tends to be the one they are most knowledgeable of and which they practice.

The mobilisation of inner awareness, the stimulation of and contact with deep healing energies, and their expression in various symbolic forms, are necessary but not always sufficient for healing to take place. Something else is required to make it effective and lasting. Many people have visions and inner guidance but these may not endure. The vital extra ingredient required is integration. All of the gains, insights, wisdom, and energy have to be integrated into a reforming personality. Character change is required; without this the initial progress is temporary and integration is not possible. By way of an example of how healing intelligence lies deep in the psyche in the middle of emotional disturbance I offer two dreams of my own from my early twenties, a time of life in which I felt disorientated, cut off from my deeper self, and in a state of emotional suffering:

> I arrive at a large house for a psychotherapy session. I notice a flood of water and the house is in danger of collapse. I rush into the basement, extract a musical manuscript, and leave just in time.

A house is often a symbol for the psyche; here was a powerful dream telling me I was in danger of collapse and a flood of emotions were bursting within me. The musical manuscript was a beautiful symbol showing there was something which I, my conscious personality, had to rescue. It symbolised, for me, spirit and feeling, precisely the parts of myself that had been lost. The healing intelligence within the psyche gave me not only an exact and powerful diagnosis of my inner world but also showed me the way forward. Two years later I had the following dream:

> I am digging in a garden; the soil is rich and dark but also tough work. My mother tells me my uncle, a Christian missionary, is visiting and I should come into the house to meet him. I decide, however, to continue digging. I become aware of a witch who has entered the garden and will pass close behind me. She is so powerful I could die in this process. I feel her, like an X-ray, penetrating me to the bone, scanning my core, as if testing me. I brace myself, bending my knees and adopt a strong stance. She passes by.

Clearly, I had progressed in these two years and the house was no longer caving in. Moreover, the ground is rich but requires a lot of energy. Faced with the task of digging into the deep psyche, my family background in the Christian church offered itself as my chief resource, symbolized by my uncle. However, I had reached a different stage in my life and was determined to do this digging alone. Instead, I was to encounter the potentially dangerous yet ultimately healing energies lying in the psyche.

Such dreams are quite common for many people in emotional and spiritual difficulty. The natural health of the psyche resists distortions imposed on it by social conditioning, harmful upbringing, traumas, emotional suffering, and often presents a picture of what is happening in the psyche in a most dramatic fashion. This can be completely different to the one constructed by the conscious mind. Moreover, healing intelligence not only presents the current state of the psyche but also offers hope and purpose, frequently showing the way forward. The task of healing is to contact this intelligence, a natural resource within the psyche, and integrate it with consciousness.

Dream analysis is a well-tried method for accessing the unconscious. However, other methods exist, such as meditative techniques, imaginal body work, active imagination, emotionally expressive techniques, light trance states, chakra work, and many more. Some of these will be explored in this book and their unifying principles elucidated. There are also other stages of the healing journey besides contacting the deep psyche—such as integration—which are essential for the full healing and individuation process.

Chapter One gives a general overview of four stages of psychotherapy incorporating a spiritual dimension. The emergence of a spiritual dimension is more typical in the later stages where transformative features in the personality occur. The main ingredients of psychotherapy with a spiritual dimension are then outlined.

Chapter Two outlines stage three of the psychotherapy journey, the alignment to the deep psyche, describing methods and concepts advocated by Jung, especially those of active imagination and the transcendent function. Other methods for accessing the unconscious are mentioned and stress is laid on the use of inner awareness, imaginal body work, and experiential focusing. A process of *Expressing—Stilling—Awakening—Locating—Approaching—Mobilising* is described.

Chapter Three examines the relationship of the therapist and client at this third stage of the process—the alignment to the deep psyche. The quality of the therapist, especially the capacity to connect to the deep psyche, is central for the client's progress. Four ways are outlined by which the psychotherapist helps the client: first, to attune to the unconscious; second, to express complexes and emotional pain; third, to clear out negative attitudes such as self-pity or depressive tendencies impeding clear access to the deeper material; fourth, to locate the healing energy lying in the psyche, and for this the quality of the healing energy of the therapist is crucial. It is useful to think of the relationship between therapist and client as a shared field.

Chapter Four gives an overview of the integration process—essential for healing to be actualised. There are three practical steps: to assess the suitability of the material arising from the unconscious; to work psychologically with the unconscious; to promote the movement towards a new centre of personality and identity. Case studies are then given showing the lengthy nature of attempts at integration as well as different capacities to integrate.

Chapter Five looks at how healing intelligence works as an inner process. The vitality of healing intelligence may be thought of as *potency*, with dynamic character features including *expressiveness and receptivity* essential for its effective functioning. The role of ego consciousness in the healing process is outlined. Six ways in which healing intelligence works in the psyche are outlined. Obstacles or resistances to it are then enumerated.

Chapter Six concerns integration with the spirit. Spiritual neglect can lead to a lessening and even crippling of the personality. Integration (linking) is required between two parts of the psyche. A synopsis of chakras is given and case studies illustrate how they might be used in psychotherapy. "Reminder" dreams are very common for spiritually minded people, which involve a linking of the ego to the higher self and allow integration and healing to take place. The chapter ends with the Gnostic tale of the Hymn of the Pearl, highlighting the integration possibilities lying within it.

Chapter Seven poses a wide range of questions on the nature of healing, with reflections and answers following. These include the relationship between healing, wholeness and religion, the existence of many sources of healing in the psyche rather than just one, how healing takes place outside psychotherapy, and how it has existed for all of human history. These summarize previous material and allow opportunities to consider wider spiritual and philosophical questions.

The model of the psyche in this book is one commonly used in depth psychotherapy of a Jungian persuasion. *Consciousness* has many functions but is centred in the ego while the *deep psyche*, a parallel term to that of the unconscious, consists of two parts: first, the *personal unconscious* where defence systems, filtering mechanisms, complexes, traumas, and accessible material are contained; second, the *collective unconscious*, which is the emotional foundation, the archetypal, spiritual functioning of a human being—this is the ultimate source of healing intelligence though it exists at all levels in the psyche. The glossary explains these terms and the reasons for their usage in more detail.

CHAPTER ONE

Psychotherapy with a spiritual dimension

Psychotherapy is a broad discipline. Even within individual schools, such as the Freudian and Jungian, there are various branches holding different views of its process. For many psychotherapists the word healing enters little into their vocabulary or training. However, some do advocate a spiritual dimension to their work, such as Existentialist and Humanist psychotherapists, others have a deep interest in it, such as Jungian schools, while others make explicit a transcendent and spiritual component to the psyche—the schools of Psychosynthesis and Transpersonal Psychology, for example. Other psychotherapists, although not trained in this area, find spiritual matters arising, yet may have few tools to continue work in this manner. This chapter gives a general overview of the process of psychotherapy incorporating a spiritual dimension. The approach outlined here is inspired by the work of Jung and is close to that envisaged by Assagioli. It also incorporates a meditative-type technique, akin to experiential focusing, which leans towards transpersonal theory and practice. Four stages of this process are outlined, with the spiritual dimension being particularly located in parts three and four. These stages are:

1. *Containment and comprehension*
2. *Analysis of character*
3. *Alignment with the deep psyche*
4. *Integration and emergence of a different centre to the personality*

Frequently, the activation of spiritual components does not occur until stage three. It is best preceded by a thorough character analysis. Bearing in mind these stages are not strictly sequential but are a broad indication of the path of an intensive psychotherapy, they are now examined briefly so as to provide a psychotherapeutic context for the emergence of spiritual work.

Containment and comprehension

Emotional suffering is the overwhelming reason for approaching psychotherapy. This can be expressed in the outer world in terms of relationship and work problems or it might be experienced mainly internally as in depression or anxiety. The variety of problems is, clearly, very large. This first stage of psychotherapy involves close attention to clients' symptoms, at first the presenting ones. It implies an admission that clients cannot go on as they are and that they require help. There is, hopefully, a growing, positive relationship between therapist and client: the working alliance. Containment of clients by the therapist is a very primary experience by which they feel held, appreciated, and understood at an emotional level. It resembles the holding and handling period of early mothering. Clients may also benefit from a process of reflection by the therapist in the following two ways: first, by seeing their problems are understood; second, by feeling their essence, true value, or real nature is in some sense being recognised, valued, and reflected back to them. Not everyone comes to therapy looking for an analysis of character. Some come to clarify a situation and wish to use the therapy to explore possibilities before acting. Such legitimate use of the therapeutic space does not necessarily require the extensive tools of depth psychotherapy. The very act of providing comprehension and containment may be enough for many clients to gain perspective on their problems and they may not need to pass to the later stages outlined below. After a limited number of sessions they should have a fair understanding of their suffering and whence it arose.

Analysis of character

In addition to efforts of understanding the presenting crisis, psychotherapy attempts to comprehend the presenting symptom in the context of the character of the client. It looks to early history and family dynamics to discover how character has been formed. It begins, therefore, to analyse the client. It has a number of tools at its disposal, including models of how human character is formed, how defence systems operate, a classification of pathology, and many more.

The client first accesses parts of the personal unconscious, typically emotions held just below the surface of consciousness, presenting themselves as complexes. This stage may be extended beyond a preliminary understanding so that a clearer understanding of the psyche, its suffering, vulnerabilities, defences, and strengths, is identified, especially within the context of the family dynamic and the client's personal history. A wider range of understanding and interpretation becomes possible. This development of self-understanding is very beneficial, especially in characters where ego strength is reasonably strong and there is no fundamental damage to the psyche. In these cases, change is easier, behaviour can be altered, relationships changed, and entrenched patterns questioned. This stage is often characterised by a reductive analysis in which the behaviour and symptoms of the clients are explained in terms of a model of psychological development and early family dynamics.

The alignment with the deep psyche

In many cases, psychotherapy does not pass beyond the above analytic stage. Much understanding may have been gained and this may be sufficient for many, who may now not only formulate strategies of how to tackle their problems but also be clearer how their character structure has contributed to their suffering. However, others may not have shifted out of the patterns of difficulty and suffering with which they came. Many reasons exist for this. Some have intense wounds that will not heal simply as a result of greater understanding: trauma at a young age, for instance, is extremely resistant to healing; the psyche becomes shaped at its very formation in response to this wound, which is not something added to an otherwise healthy psyche, but rather becomes an integral part of it. Another reason might be that ego consciousness is controlling the therapy, conducting it intellectually, continually attempting to understand the causes of the problem. In these cases the dominance of the ego needs to be questioned and replaced with a closer relationship to the unconscious. Repressive mechanisms and resistance can be strong.

The deep psyche links to the emotional foundation, the archetypal and spiritual functioning of a human being. (Where it touches the numinous, the transcendent, it may be thought of as soul). At these levels, love, sexuality, and spirit are all operative. This third stage, unlike previous ones, cannot be learnt by normal methods. It requires an art, best developed by allowing the energies of the unconscious to emerge and subsequently cooperating with them.

The psychotherapist's task, at this stage, is to help the client orientate the ego to this deeper psyche. Within Jungian psychotherapy many methods are used in order to access it, the most well known being dream work. Other methods, such as transference work, challenge the ego's defences: for instance, through the emergence of frustration or despair directed towards the therapist who may contain the build-up of such emotions and then help the client understand this as a projection of a childhood complex. The dominance of the ego needs to be questioned. Jung even spoke of using, in extreme cases, hypnogogic methods to achieve this (*CW*, Vol. 8, para. 83), by which he means light trance states which bypass the ego and lie between the state of wakefulness and sleep, examples of which will be given throughout this book. As deeper complexes are brought into consciousness and modified, the psyche becomes less burdened by them and there is a closer relationship to the unconscious.

The method of all depth psychotherapy dealing with the unconscious is to work with deeper emotions, complexes, and traumas and seek their expression in consciousness. What distinguishes the Jungian point of view (indeed most psychotherapy of a spiritual orientation) is the overarching hypothesis of a directing centre (or centres) outside of the ego, in the deep psyche.

As opposed to stage two (which Jung called analytic or reductive), stage three he describes as synthetic or constructive since it brings together different parts of the psyche and looks to the future. Assagioli describes this stage as realisation of the true centre. Here, both therapist and client are no longer principally trying to understand or analyse but are engaging with the deeper psyche, listening to and learning from its way of communicating through symbols, dramatic scenes, tales, images, and puns. Such a method uses metaphor rather than logic; it circles around a problem until its meaning naturally reveals itself; it does not primarily use thinking and sensation functions but rather intuition and feeling; it works better with multiple meanings and ambivalences. At this stage, the client begins to express the deeper psyche more forcibly, to appreciate its archetypal and transformative elements, to have new visions of life and to connect to it more deeply. Consciousness is now more closely linked to the deeper psyche. Here transformation begins and healing energy is contacted.

Integration and the emergence of a different centre to the personality

The descent into the unconscious can transform the personality to an extent, depending not only on how rich has been the experience but also on how the deeper material has been integrated. For this to happen a process of character development must occur, otherwise the process remains ungrounded and any gains will be temporary. Integration and the emergence of a different centre to the personality go hand in hand.

The reforming personality may then shift from its original position to a new one which is some way between the Self and the ego. The Self is understood here as an inner directing centre within the deep psyche.

It is difficult to be dogmatic about the concept of Self, about whether it is a singular central archetype or the totality of the psyche. In this book it is used in the former sense as the inner director, the organizing principle, the archetype of order as Fordham (1957) called it. The expression deep psyche, used frequently in these pages, is a parallel term to the unconscious, in which the Self is acknowledged as the archetype of order, but in addition to which there are multiple centres of healing intelligence, like chakras in the psyche.

In summary, with respect to the above stages: all four are experienced in a complete psychotherapy. The first lays the foundation, establishing the conditions for trust and the working alliance; the second stage of analysis brings knowledge of character including its emotional and unconscious determinants; the third stage of alignment to the deep psyche shifts the centre of personality towards the deeper psyche and the Self; the fourth, integration, the creative uniting of the deep psyche and consciousness is crucial, enabling the previous stages to be converted to gains.

This whole journey has been called the individuation process and constitutes the spiritual journey championed by Jungian analysts. Such work of expanding consciousness, from its initial, limited and defended position to this more developed one, is often experienced in spiritual terms since work in the unconscious has archetypal components that bestow the energy of transformation and healing. The realms of spirit and deep psyche have been interlinked throughout Jungian thought. Stein comments that this process

> is able more completely to represent a person's wholeness in all its heights and depths, from the instinctual to the spiritual—body, soul and spirit ... a person is freed to be himself fully, freely and genuinely. The whole individual changes ... this irrational process of individuation is a deeply spiritual one since the contents that emerge from the unconscious are typically numinous.

> (Stein, 2005, pp. 11–12)

The idea that psychotherapy consists of different stages is intuitively obvious to any practitioner. The stages of the process outlined by the school of Psychosynthesis (Assagioli, 1965, p. 21) are similar to those outlined in this book. They are first, analysis of character, second, control of its elements, third, realisation of the true centre, fourth, psychosynthesis, the formation or reconstruction of the personality around a new centre. Assagioli also puts stress on the higher self as essential to the transformative process.

Besides the analytic/synthetic distinction given by Jung (a two-part structure of the psychotherapy journey), on another occasion he outlined four stages of the process: Confession, Elucidation, Education, and Transformation (*CW*, Vol. 5, para. 122). He described the first two stages in some detail. Confession refers to the revealing of the patient's secrets and suffering, with particular emphasis on the shadow, while Elucidation refers to the stage of analysis with its emphasis on reductive understanding of emotional suffering in the "family drama". Education refers to the lessons learnt from the earlier stages being applied to social and external situations, while Transformation refers to the concomitant change in the personality, the object of the journey. Besides this generic and early vision (1929), Jung, at other times, gave a more specific outline of the stages of psychotherapy or the individuation process—a fundamental reordering of the personality around a new centre. This begins with an examination of the personal unconscious, proceeds to examine the persona, the shadow, the anima/animus, and leads to the integration of the Self.

The four stages outlined in this chapter are close then to those envisioned by Assagioli and Jung with respect to the psychotherapy process but there are some modifications. First, here the stage of integration is highly emphasised. It often does not get the same coverage as the more dramatic accounts of the descent and the encounter with the unconscious but without it there is no sustained transformation. Both Jung and Assagioli appreciated, of course, that such integration is a process of character reform. Since this "moral" dimension is of such importance to both psychotherapy and spiritual development later chapters will examine more thoroughly what integration, as a practical process, actually means. Second, I place less emphasis on specific archetypal components, such as anima and animus, although the central principle of contact with an archetypal layer of the deep psyche is maintained since this is where healing intelligence originates. Other central Jungian concepts such as the shadow and the Self have been retained and held as being of the highest importance.

Such an individuation journey has been criticised as highly individualistic, perhaps cutting the client off from the world of social relations, cocooning him in an individual philosophy based on purely personal development. However, psychotherapists who work with a spiritual dimension are well aware that the stages of life, with their social and intimate relations, are of the utmost importance. What can be appropriate for a fifty-year-old may be most unsuitable for a young adult. Teenagers generally need to realize themselves in their peer group and establish their identity—an isolationist philosophy is rarely of use to them. A thirty-year-old may have marriage as his next rite of passage; his path of development may require relationship, courtship and reproduction. The next stage may be parenthood, responsibility, and so on. Individuation, broadly conceived, requires individuals to pass through their stages of development in order to fulfil themselves. Proper therapy will help them face their rites of passage and progress to the next stage of development and many of these stages are in a socially related context. Neither is it accurate to say all individuals pass through the same stages. Some will have unique destinies quite unlike those of the general population. For these, too, a thorough analysis is most useful since this uniqueness is valued, developed, and integrated by such a process.

The above model—stages one to four of the psychotherapy journey—is a generic one. There are many exceptions to this notion of a developmental goal or individuation process and many useful things can be accomplished by psychotherapy without completing its later stages as outlined here. Understanding can be advanced, consciousness raised, and relationships improved without resort to the numinous or archetypal aspects of healing. Improved ego functioning, greater intellectual understanding of one's problems, encouragement of greater control or moderation—all have their place in attempts to improve human character. All this might be said to belong to the earlier stages. In brief, the complete individuation journey is an ideal to which there are many exceptions. It is not the sole purpose of coming to therapy.

At the other end of the spectrum some practitioners, perhaps in a spiritual group with a psychotherapeutic orientation, may concentrate on stage three, the alignment to the deep psyche, while giving little importance to stages one and two. They may believe in the power of spirit, a higher self, or God with such conviction that the mundane task of analysing character can seem at best a waste of time or at worst an indulgence in victim psychology. Not for them is the painstaking work at the base of the mountain of individuation, struggling with complexes, character formation, and interpersonal difficulties. They focus on the rarefied heights of the summit—transformation and archetypal experience. Rather than flounder at the base of this mountain, or risk hubris (like Icarus' flight in the heavens), the more productive perspective, I believe, is to embrace both ends of this spectrum, engaging in the solid task of character analysis while searching for transformational, spiritual energy as well as promoting integration. So what is distinctive about such psychotherapy?

First, psychotherapy with a spiritual dimension will, when appropriate, pass to the later stages of alignment to the deep psyche and integration. Understanding is not enough, transformation is the goal, healing is its path.

Second, since it is more purposive and less reductive than a more traditional psychotherapy this work with a spiritual dimension values the earlier stages rather differently. It may not reduce a neurosis to childhood dynamics but places more emphasis on the current crisis and its opportunities to reshape character so as to lead a more fruitful and fulfilled life. The unlocking of potentiality leads to the future and the next stage of development.

Third, psychotherapy with a spiritual dimension has a view of the psyche in which spiritual components are not to be explained away as defences but are regarded as vital components of health. A connection to the deeper or higher self is an asset in the healing journey.

Fourth, the style of the therapy is not primarily analytic, with its emphasis on understanding the unconscious, its complexes and dynamics, but synthetic, which rather aligns to the deep psyche and learns its symbolic language and metaphorical expression. There is a letting go, a surrendering of the dominance of ego-based consciousness. It is the alignment of the ego to the deep psyche, especially the establishing of a healthy ego-Self axis (Edinger, 1972; Neumann, 1988), that is the start of the transformative process. Some of the methods described later suggest that temporary suspensions of normal consciousness are beneficial in accessing the unconscious. Once this work has begun it is the integration of the material from the unconscious that provides the new viewpoint, energy, and vision leading to the reform of the ego.

Both the conscious personality and the unconscious are changed in this encounter and integration experience. The ego, the conscious perspective, and personality components associated with it, are modified by the meeting with the deeper psyche. On the other hand, the energies of the unconscious are released: the Self, now recognised, is freer and there can be a sense of joy at this experience. The shadow, the darker side of personality, previously repressed, is now more integrated and its energies incorporated into the ego; other repressed or neglected components of the personality may be incorporated and thus the psyche is more harmonious. On a metaphysical note, a Jungian/Gnostic interpretation on this point might suggest that God (roughly translated as archetype of the Self) and man (roughly translated as ego) need one another equally: the ego needs to be transformed by the Self, but the Self needs the individualised, differentiated ego to know itself, to become conscious. Otherwise the self remains unconscious.

While healing intelligence exists in the psyche one should be aware of the limits of psychotherapy and not suppose that total healing is a guaranteed result. Jung comments:

> There is a widespread prejudice that analysis is something like a "cure" to which one submits for a time and is then discharged healed. This is layman's error left over from the early days of psychoanalysis .... There are very few cases where a single "cure" is permanently successful.

> (CW, Vol. 8, para. 142)

Rather he describes the process as one of "readjustment of the psychological attitude" and moreover this "adaptation is never achieved once and for all" but each stage of life has new challenges (ibid. 143); a thorough analysis provides an important platform from which to face these.

The above-mentioned four stages are presented as a sequence for the purposes of clarity of exposition; there are many exceptions to it. However, all stages should be developed by one means or another otherwise the healing and individuation process is unbalanced or incomplete. If at any point the psychotherapy falters or stagnates it is useful to ask at which of the above stages the problem lies and then seek solutions appropriate to that stage.

Psychotherapy with a spiritual dimension involves all four stages of psychotherapy, the early ones being preparatory and foundational for later progress. As presented here such psychotherapy has transpersonal potential. The deep psyche has both higher (spiritual) and lower (instinctual) components. An integrative approach involves both ends of the psychic spectrum, each needing the other for an experience of wholeness to occur.

CHAPTER TWO

Alignment of consciousness to the deep psyche

Four broad stages of the psychotherapeutic journey have been outlined and it is in the third and fourth that, more typically, a spiritual dimension emerges, depending on the potential within the client and the experience of the therapist. Since so much has been written on the first two stages, especially the analysis of character, these will not be covered here but only mentioned to give a context for the work that follows. This is not to downplay the early stages since they provide the essential foundation for the later ones. Bearing this in mind, this chapter will examine the third of these, the alignment process.

Contacting and working with the deep psyche—Jung's method

To contact the spiritual energies of the psyche it is vital to listen to the inner world, to be in touch with what it is trying to communicate. Such listening is intense connectedness. The theoretical template for the healing methods and processes described in this book have their origins in the work of Jung and specifically his 1916 essay *The Transcendent Function* (CW, Vol. 8), which sketches an outline of psychotherapy as he understood it at that time. In it the transcendent function is presented as the union of the conscious with the unconscious. He outlines two broad methodologies—the analytic and the synthetic—locating the latter in the second half of the work. To find ways of contacting the unconscious it is necessary not just to analyse it reductively but to work with its synthetic, synergistic, multilayered, and constructive character and respect its purposive, future-looking function:

> Constructive treatment of the unconscious, that is the question of meaning and purpose, paves the way for the patient's insight into the process which I call the transcendent function.
>
> (CW, Vol. 8, para. 147)

Jung poses two practical questions: first, how does the practitioner help the patient overcome the gap between the unconscious and consciousness? Second, having accessed the contents of the unconscious, what is the best way of working with them?

With respect to the first question—contacting the unconscious—Jung considers dreams and concludes that "they are unsuitable or difficult to make use of in developing the transcendent function, because they make too great demands upon the subject" (ibid. 153). Rather he suggests, instead, the method of immersion in the emotional complex, the use of hypnogogic states and active imagination. This point, somewhat surprising coming from Jung, is, nevertheless, understandable. It is possible to "drown" in dream material, while other methods can be more direct, since the active participation of consciousness with the content of the unconscious has more experiential immediacy and impact than the more removed method of dream analysis. However, in the broad sweep of his life's work, dreams are treated as of great value for the transformation process and, combined with the above methods, are very effective.

He then considers the use of "unconscious inferences" or "ideas out the blue", lapses of memory, slips, and the like, but considers these to be more suited to reductive rather than constructive methods (ibid. 154). He next mentions "spontaneous fantasies", which are evidently useful, but not everyone can produce them and, "where this is the case, special measures are required" (ibid. 155). Jung appreciates the need for original methods, where appropriate, and proposes, in the above cases where phantasies are not forthcoming, to "resort to special aid" (ibid. 166). He is also well aware that the use of unusual techniques has dangers since these unconscious contents "may overpower the conscious mind and take possession of the personality" (CW, Vol. 8, p. 67).

Jung proceeds to explain his central technique to contact the unconscious, suggesting the patient should first immerse himself in his emotional complex:

> In the intensity of the emotional disturbance itself lies the value, the energy which he should have at his disposal in order to remedy the state of reduced adaptation. Nothing is achieved by repressing this state or devaluing it rationally … he must make himself as conscious as possible of the mood he is in, sinking himself in it without reserve … fantasy must be allowed the freest possible play … the whole procedure is a kind of enrichment of and clarification of the affect … this work by itself can have a favorable and vitalizing influence … this is the beginning of the transcendent function, i.e., of the collaboration of the conscious and unconscious data.

> (CW, Vol. 8, para. 167)

Jung further suggests ways of elaborating the unconscious contents by drawing and using one's hands to give expression to the unconscious (ibid. 168). The main task is that "critical attention must be eliminated" (ibid. 170), that is, the ego must be bypassed. He recommends hypnogogic methods, by which voices can be heard or images seen, that elaborate the contents of the unconscious.

His answer to the second question—of how to work these contents, once elicited—is that it requires a balance between their creative elaboration and the development of their meaning. As this dual process proceeds, the ego, which has been in abeyance up to this point, is now brought in with equal importance to the unconscious. Its position and attitude now becomes part of the equation and there is a meeting between the two opposites of consciousness and the deep psyche. The confrontation with the unconscious, the dialogue with inner archetypal figures at the core of complexes, is a major method of this process. "The shuttling to and fro of arguments and affects represents the transcendent function of opposites" (ibid. 188). In the prefatory note to this 1958 essay Jung mentions that while this technique is the "most important auxiliary for the production of those contents of the unconscious" nevertheless it has dangers since it can easily turn into the Freudian free association method "wherein the patient gets stuck in the sterile circle of his complexes" or becomes fascinated with their aesthetic aspects.

Such techniques led to the method of active imagination since essentially they involved not passive observation of the contents of the unconscious but a direct relationship with them. *The Red Book* (2009), with Jung's personal revelations of his inner struggle, makes clear that an active dialogue with the figures from the inner world was his favored method, along with dream analysis, of contacting and engaging the unconscious. These figures, such as Philemon and Elijah, could be talked to, even challenged; the inner world is regarded as totally real and the ego can engage in creative dialogue with the soul.

The later stages of analysis involve, then, the activation of what Jung called the transcendent function. If one thinks of the client's pre-therapy position as one in which the ego and the Self are at two ends of an axis through which there is little communication and upon which the centre of personality is located in the camp of the ego, then a fruitful post-therapy position is one in which this axis is now far more alive to the interaction between ego and the Self. It is a healthier axis upon which the centre of the personality is located somewhere in-between these two positions. This new centre of awareness, the transcendent function, can listen to both positions, though identifying with neither; it can transcend the position of the ego and can build a ladder to the Self. It differentiates itself from the powerful influence of both poles: on the one hand from the influence of the outside world and its pressures to conform, and on the other the fascination with the depths of the unconscious. The centre of gravity now shifts. This is very different to a full-blown spiritual position which might recommend a supposed abolishment of the ego and identification with the Self. Also it differs from the position which overemphasizes control of the ego over the deeper reaches of the unconscious. While this individuation process, at some point, bypasses ego consciousness in order to access the deep psyche, it does not advocate a dismantling of the ego, which paradoxically is relativized but strengthened at the same time. It is relativized since it is no longer the centre of the personality yet it is strengthened as it is no longer assailed to the same extent by complexes and opposite forces in the unconscious. The experience of healing strengthens the foundations and therefore the superstructure, the ego, is in better condition. Kohut (1984), for instance, highlights four possible beneficial results of the psychotherapeutic process: empathy, humour, creativity, and wisdom.

The transcendent function, therefore, represents a middle position between the ego and the unconscious, a capacity to listen to both positions though identifying with neither. The Latin word *transcendere* means to climb across or pass over. It is a position which links the two opposites of consciousness and unconsciousness in the psyche. (For fuller discussion of the communality of Kohut's and Jung's ideas on the outcomes of psychotherapy, Jabobi (1990, pp. 113–149) has an enlightening commentary.)

Jung's method of contacting the unconscious and working with it can be understood partially as a creative reaction to the Freudian methods which he adopted in his early practice. Freud's influence over the early psychoanalytic movement was, of course, immense and Jung's separation produced in him a both a breakdown and breakthrough (see Field (1996) for an interesting overview of this topic). It was by the working through of his personal crisis and addressing the collective crisis of his age that Jung developed new theories and methodologies for working with the psyche. Thus, he began to stress the direct encounter with the emotional complex, rather than simply analysing it. He emphasized methods for suspending the analytic, thinking mind, the interfering, controlling ego while collaborating with, rather than always interpreting, the unconscious. The role of the authoritative, analytical doctor who provided interpretations was replaced by a very different philosophy in which the ego was transformed by temporarily diminishing its power and control. The unconscious, instead of being viewed as a repressive storehouse, became rather an inner guiding system which transmitted messages via symbols which were akin to those in fairy tales, dreams, and mythology. This is a new synthetic, rather than just analytic, method of working with the unconscious and was therefore distinct from the psychoanalytic tradition.

Inner awareness—a method for contacting and working with the deep psyche

Jung developed many transpersonal components in his efforts to align consciousness to the unconscious. However, one method that seemed absent was a practice of meditation. Active imagination may have been ideally suited to Jung's temperament: he was a man of volcanic creativity and courageous attitude, whose inner world could flood him. However, this may not be a suitable method for those of a more delicate disposition or less in contact with a tumultuous inner world. The healer, in innovating new methods, of course uses the ones that have worked for him. They might also work for those of similar disposition or those who were directly influenced by him. Meditational awareness and related practices became a lot more common in the West in the second half of the twentieth century and their value as an aid to deeper psychotherapy and spiritual work has been accepted by some practitioners and writers. Vaughan (1986) and Welwood (2006), for example, both give excellent accounts of how they incorporate these in their psychotherapy practice. Jung's injunction that Western people should remain true to their own traditions has not been generally followed even by Jungian analysts, who have generally become very tolerant and global with respect to their spiritual sustenance.

In the spirit of Jung's creative methods for contacting the contents of the unconscious, but also in line with the use of meditational-type practices within psychotherapy, this chapter illustrates a method that can be used under certain conditions. It has a focusing-awareness technique, which at its most simple includes listening to the deep psyche, expressing honestly and forcibly whatever pain or complexes lie within it, and contacting the dark and light aspects of the psyche.

Although incorporating simple Eastern techniques, it is similar to the methods elaborated in *The Transcendent Function*. It has a meditative-type structure to begin with—not used by Jung as far as I am aware—and then passes on to an experiential focusing method (Gendlin, 1981). Three principles underlie this technique:

1. Healing takes place by the mobilization of inner awareness. It begins with stillness and pure awareness, progressing to an awareness of emotional pain.
2. Pain and trauma can be accessed through body centers. This can prove not only cathartic but also bring new energy, information, and feelings allowing the ego to readjust.
3. In addition, there can be a meeting, a dialogue, with and between these centres in the unconscious, thus promoting healing.

Indications of its use include the following: when other psychotherapy methods have been exhausted and progress is blocked; when the client, after being properly informed about this procedure and its risks, wishes to proceed; when the psychotherapist judges the client will not be destabilized; when clients have the capacity to benefit from such a method. Those with a creative nature or genuine spiritual background may be among these.

If the psychotherapist is unsure of the client's ability to engage with such work it is possible to have lighter experiments testing capacity, stability, and willingness to proceed with such a process. The therapist should know the journey is not recommended for everyone and be aware of counter recommendations. Supervision by an experienced practitioner, who has professional experience in this field, is advisable. Certainly, great care has to be taken not to engage in such a procedure with clients who may be destabilised, have a history of psychosis, borderline condition, or severe trauma. Caution needs to be exercised by the practitioner and the safety of the client has to be foremost; it should not be indulged in lightly or recommended indiscriminately. Jung suggests, in the preface to *The Transcendent Function*, that such methods are … "an invaluable auxiliary for the psychotherapist" but "may even lead to psychotic interval" (*CW*, Vol. 8, p. 68). The essence of the focusing–awareness process is:

> *Expressing—Stilling—Awakening—Locating—Approaching—
> Mobilising*

These steps will now be explained in more detail.

Expressing

The process of alignment, here called the scan (explained below), best begins by a direct, clear, and honest expression of the emotional pain which is not analysed but simply felt and expressed. Within the pain (or complex) is a truth which can only be reached by expressing such pain directly and forcibly. To use the vocabulary of Hillman (1975, p. 104): "within the affliction is a complex, within the complex an arche-type". The archetypal realm holds the healing potential. Within suffer-ing lies the truth of its own healing. This process corresponds to what Jung implied by the immersion in the emotional complex (*CW*, Vol. 8, para. 167) after which the transformative energy of the unconscious can be contacted.

Stillness

The stilling process is the leaving aside of those aspects of mind in which planning, worrying, desiring, organizing, assessing, filtering, and judging are involved. The desire to understand and control must be put aside. The analytic style ends and the emotional, intuitive, syn-thetic parts of the mind are freed. Thus, the analytic and judging mind is on "standby". It is not exactly switched off; it can be re-activated very quickly, but the normal functions of mind are given very little energy. This state is peaceful but very alert to the inner world. This stage cor-responds to what Jung meant by "critical attention must be eliminated" (ibid. 170). This part of the scan is, then, akin to a meditation expe-rience. Breathing techniques are used. Focusing on the in-breath and out-breath is a simple method. However, any method which stills the normal mind is useful.

Awakening

The key to the scan is the awakening and maintenance of inner aware-ness. Vaughan (1986) calls this type of awareness "healing awareness", Welwood (2006) calls it "unconditional presence". It has also been termed the witness state. This meditational state is one of an alert yet initially non-focused awareness. It is often done with the eyes closed, sitting upright but can also be practiced lying down. The task is to let this awareness be activated, and a reliable, fast way of doing this is by focusing on the breath. The normal, conscious mind having relaxed and receded, the process may begin. Just as the analysing mind has needed to retire, so too, strong emotions such as fear or anger should not take over the inner awareness which has now developed. Breathing techniques, focusing on the in-breath and out-breath, are again valuable at this point. By returning to the breath, perhaps by encouragement of the therapist, the client regains calmness and so learns not to be overwhelmed by this powerful world of emotion. This is not the awareness of the normal mind that has been put on standby. Normal consciousness has been suspended so another awareness can awaken. In inner awareness there is an absence of analysing, judgement, filtering, avoidance, shame, guilt, or anger. It is pure inner awareness as in meditation. It has no agenda, theories, or intellectualisms. It does not preconceive what this pain is or where it comes from. It simply experiences it in the present, as it is, un-interpreted. This state is one where awareness functions unimpeded by ego consciousness.

Location of emotional suffering

With the eyes closed, the remaining senses become acute. Turning inwards the client is now on the verge of approaching the inner world. The body can be thought of as a map of the unconscious and within it lies any emotional pain, which is therefore registered in a symbolic or imaginal body, as it were. It is nevertheless felt as "real" there in the body, such as love in the heart, excitement in the chest, fear in the stomach. Once the process of contacting and expressing such emotions begins one can start to work directly with the unconscious. This first step is the honest encounter with emotional pain as it is felt in the body rather than in the conscious mind. Therefore, at this point, the therapist can ask the client where in her body she feels the emotional pain of which she has been talking. She may reply she feels it in her throat, chest, heart, or stomach. An honest encounter with one's inner world is central to all psychotherapeutic endeavour. What distinguishes the method at this stage of the therapy is that it is done in an inner meditative state with ego consciousness largely suspended.

Approach

The next step is to approach and remain with this pain by means of one's inner awareness. By this time in the scan, awareness of the outer world has diminished considerably for the client. The inner reality, intensely experienced at this point, is the total focus. No one at this stage of the journey doubts the reality of what is felt and experienced. Before the scan it was possible for the client to say … "Well, maybe, I feel this, I am not sure." Here there is no doubt about real feelings.

Mobilising

If the client can, with her awareness, stay with the pain in this honest encounter then healing energies may be contacted and activated. Naturally there are cases of trauma, for instance, when such catharsis is not available to the psyche and the deeper work may not take place—an alternative therapeutic style then needs to be used. However, when activated these healing energies include the following possibilities:

1. Cathartic feelings may be released by this contact between awareness and repressed emotion. This is an important first sign of healing and its absence indicates that further progress may be difficult or impossible.
2. Communication from the area of pain to the faculty of inner awareness of the nature of the pain—whence it arose, how the client has maintained this state of affairs, and the nature of resistances. This may be done in symbolic form and require interpretation after the scan.
3. The arousal of healing energy. This can be done from two sources: first, from within the area of the emotional wound itself, providing it still has enough health and energy; second, from another area of the deep psyche—for instance, the heart or the area of spiritual intuition (brow chakra) can heal emotional wounds in other parts of the psyche.
4. An indication of the way forward. Frequently, healing intelligence shows the subject the way forward out of the present impasse, usually in symbolic form.

This remarkable inner wisdom and healing force may now be released. It is the same inner, purposive intelligence as in significant dreams. The difference is the immediacy of the process described here and the direct active participation of awareness in this process.

Other therapists have described this process in comparable terms. "Healing awareness" has been described by Frances Vaughan (1985, p. 59) as an available option for the therapist which "is a non-interfering attention that allows natural self-healing responses to take place" and which can be "consciously cultivated"; for her it is an awareness especially identified with the higher self. Welwood (1983, p. 44) outlines how the "felt sense is a wider way our body holds or 'knows' many aspects of a situation all at once—sub-verbally, holistically, intuitively. It is concretely *felt*—in the body—as a *sense*—something not yet clear or distinct". Following Gendlin (1981) he refers to the type of awareness required as "experiential focusing within the context of existential therapy", distinguishing this from "mindfulness meditation within the context of Buddhist psychology" Welwood (1983, p. 44). He highlights a four-part healing process (Welwood, 2006, p. 78)—*Acknowledging, Allowing, Opening* and *Entering*—centred around the power of deep awareness in the psyche—comparable to the process outlined earlier in this chapter. To illustrate this in more detail there now follow two case studies.

Case study. Michael: working with dark, experiencing light

Michael was a talented composer in his mid twenties, without a partner. He felt very elevated by the world of music but was wracked by promiscuous activity. He was profoundly doubtful of his capacity to have a loving intimate relationship with a woman; nevertheless, somewhere he felt it was possible for him. His early journey in psychotherapy involved confession of his shadow, especially its sexual aspects. Yet, while wishing for these activities to stop, the psychotherapy at first remained superficial because he was unable to take a different attitude towards these parts of himself, which he regarded as reprehensible and felt he should avoid—but couldn't. His psyche was therefore severely divided between his elevated music and his lower, compulsive promiscuity. A year passed with no breakthrough. We were stuck, despair set in and the crisis was reached.

The breakthrough stage of our work began with imaginal body work, which involves locating one's emotional pain in the body. With the crisis and despair, a willingness to try new methods emerged. He became able to lie down on the couch. The new stage of the work started at its most simple, calming his mind using straightforward breathing techniques and awakening his inner awareness. Then I could ask, "Where is it you feel pain?" "Here", he pointed to the centre of his chest. "Can you describe it?" I ask. "And now can you speak from the pain without interpretation? Just tell me the way it is. Can you speak of it in the first person?" Speaking directly in the first person is a simple but useful technique to express emotional pain. Instead of the conscious mind looking at the pain from a distance and saying "*I think* I feel such and such ... " or saying "*It* feels like such and such", awareness now shifts from the ego to the area of pain and speaks directly from within it. It says "*I* feel such and such." In other words, the "I" that is referred to is no longer the conscious mind but the painful complex itself that now speaks directly and in the first person. The ease or difficulty of doing this is a strong indication for prognosis, the possibility, or not, of progress. This facility, for Michael, took some weeks to develop, oscillating in and out of ordinary analytic work.

Michael sank into the unconscious through his neglected emotional body where trauma lay. He located his pain of primal insecurity in his stomach area. It spoke directly of pain, grief, loneliness, and bewildering rage. He expressed these emotions in which he was a child lost in a strange land. The ability to concretise one's emotional pain in symbolic form is an expressive, creative, and often cathartic advance. One year into the psychotherapy he dreamt:

> A tsunami has occurred and left devastation everywhere. Many
> people all around are dead or dying. I see a young boy floating on
> the water and rescue him.

The archetype of the lost or endangered child is ubiquitous in the world's fairy tales, myths, and religions. It is also a common motif in dreams, especially of those who undergo the journey of personal development. It signifies not a real child but a symbolic one, endangered or lost, inside the dreamer. In his emotional foundations, his unconscious, a catastrophe has occurred of which his consciousness is now becoming aware. Coming to therapy has brought to his attention that something vital inside himself needs to be rescued or it will die. Here Michael makes tremendous progress and recues his inner, endangered child. He felt the child represented his potential for close relationship, something he had lost in his childhood. The child archetype may also represent the future, hope, growth, our most natural self lost on the road to adulthood.

On examining his shadow and the way he acted out his sexuality, instead of something reprehensible we found someone simply trying to end his isolation and seek tenderness and love—except he was doing it in a distorted form, protecting himself from emotional engagement. This realisation did not produce immediate change but had to be worked with, lost, and recovered. Bitter tears and strong emotional expression were vital for the journey.

Not only did he require a more natural relation to others but he eventually realized the need to completely own and take care of this lost child at the root of his shadow, for it was this inner loneliness and division in him which was fuelling his sexual acting out. This required a radical change in his life, a questioning of the split in his psyche between the higher and the lower, an attempt to break from his sexual obsessions, and a search for relationship and love. It was preceded and accompanied by many dreams which became increasingly understood once the emotional content of his shadow had been realized experientially and powerfully.

While his dreams had an impact on Michael, their interpretation was frequently disputed in the early period. What proved to be more immediately effective was our effort to directly contact his emotions and allow their forceful expression. The dreams later added weight to his growing realisation of the truth of his condition. The first stage then, in this process, was a movement by an inner awareness to honestly contact and express the repressed pain by contacting the body centres. The second stage was the emergence of awareness from within the unconscious (within the body centre), in this case from the depths of the shadow, which began to communicate. This clearly lies outside the ego because so frequently it has positions and attitudes contrary to those held by ordinary consciousness.

The difference between this type of method of working with the unconscious and that of dream interpretation is that the former is so vital and alive; interpretation becomes undeniable, inner awareness is participating in the drama. Nevertheless the dreams were very important in demonstrating to Michael his real situation and dilemmas. Dream and vision material at best coincide, giving therapist and client a sense of security that they are on the right path.

As a result of his experience of this work Michael did proceed to change his life, seek genuine relationship, and concretely change the conditions which gave rise to his repressed personality. Before the deeper work could take place it was important we had covered the ground of character analysis, family history, complexes, and the like. Also our relationship had to be tested to provide a secure basis for the descent. As important as these preliminary elements were, they were not sufficient to transform Michael from within. They were a platform. It was only the deeper work which could do that.

Michael's case shows that mobilisation of healing energies using this method can be effective. It is a two-way model demonstrating a dynamic between inner awareness on the one hand and the area of pain and repression on the other.

There now follows another case of someone who had been in psychotherapy for many years and had long-standing character problems which prevented her from progressing, especially in emotional relationships. Here, one observes a more complicated dynamic, a three-way model, in which there is a movement of energy and healing between areas of the deep psyche itself as well as with the faculty of inner awareness.

Case study. Patricia: despair and inner love

Patricia, a social worker in her forties, had suffered early abandonment trauma leaving strong emotional wounds preventing intimacy in later life. Her personality was secluded and paranoid. She had a history of broken relationships yet still wished to have a close relationship with a man. After one year's therapy we stopped talking in our accustomed way, since she felt stuck. I suggested she lie on the couch, a position encouraging a more introspective, day-dream state. She had a background of spiritual practice and expressed a need for a different form of exploration of her problems, one avoiding "mind-work". On the couch she was willing to suspend this mind dominance and through the type of breath work already mentioned she entered into a deeper state. She talked of the emotional pain in her stomach which had been there, in some way, all her life. With her inner awareness she then went into a space which was full of awful pain and gruesome images. "Now what?" she asked despairingly. I admitted we had been to this emotional area before, but to no avail since there had been no catharsis—the first good omen one looks for. However, she had always valued spiritual connection, so I asked her where she felt God was; she pointed straight to her heart with certainty. That was good, I felt, since locating feelings in the body is central in this work. "Is that where you feel love?" I asked. "Yes", she replied. I reminded her of her recent series of dreams on love so we could link up to them and reinforce this positive theme.

The experience of this inner state deepened. "Now you may do something simple", I suggested. "Be aware of the two areas simultaneously, then let the heart approach your pain area". This took about ten minutes. The atmosphere became more peaceful and still. There was no need for further intervention at this point since it was clear she was contacting her deeper psyche. On coming out of it she remembered little, so we went over the experience, recovering the material, helping her to hold on to it. The essential steps of the journey can be observed as follows:

1. Preliminary work on central complexes; a questioning of the ego structure and its defences; knowledge of the subject's history and vulnerabilities; exploration of emotional states immediately below consciousness; assessment undertaken and agreed between psychotherapist and client; a working alliance and trust.
2. A crisis point in which the ego was ready to give up its dominance; the suspension of the everyday conscious mind; the mobilising of inner awareness; imaginal body work; a meeting with the pain and its emotional expression.
3. In this case, unlike that of Michael, there was no catharsis on contacting this emotional pain. Hence, there was no immediate access to healing energies, the pain and trauma being too great. Since she wished to continue I encouraged the search for a new centre in the heart area where healing might be activated.
4. The coming together of these two centres: the movement of the healing centre (the heart) towards, and being in proximity to, the other centre (the stomach) which contained the emotional pain.
5. The alleviation of emotional pain and some measure of healing taking place.
6. The later integration of this material allowing psychological gains to be consolidated.

Healing in psychotherapy rarely takes place instantaneously. Once healing energies are mobilised (a difficult enough task in itself) there is usually a substantial period of integration required in order to consolidate long-term gains. However, the results of such experiences described above can include a considerable measure of healing, modification of complexes, an enhanced sense of self, greater feeling of authenticity, and the bettering of social and personal relationships. In the case of Patricia the result over the next few weeks was a loosening of the shadow material, an alleviation of paranoia, a less defended position vis-à-vis a potential boyfriend, and a desire to repeat the experience of this encounter with her deeper psyche. For someone like Patricia, who had early traumas, the use of this method was possible because of her spiritual background, our solid relationship, and extensive work on her inner world. In addition, there is my intervention at a critical juncture, the suggestion of activating another healing centre, the heart. Chronic emotional pain in the lower stomach usually indicates primal insecurity, a failure or serious problems with the early attachment relationship. For this reason it is important to find another area of the deep psyche which has the strength and healing properties to effect change in the area of primal insecurity. The psychotherapist's intervention is to help the natural, but un-activated, healing intelligence in the psyche. While short-term improvements in mood, diminution of suffering, and feelings of well-being can be remarkable, it is the long-term benefits that are most desired and require integrative work.

Both Michael and Patricia proved capable of really listening, specifically to their pain as it expressed itself powerfully from their inner worlds. It was necessary to suspend normal everyday consciousness and, especially, the analytic mind in order to access these feelings directly. Within the complex of Michael's pain there was a light which became more powerful and was capable of changing his attitude, his relationship to the unconscious, and eventually his life. In the case of Patricia a similar pattern could be observed: a suspension of normal consciousness, a listening to the inner world with an intense inner awareness, and an expression of the content of the painful complexes in a direct manner. In her case it was necessary to look further in her psyche to find a source of light or healing to help the damaged parts of her psyche. In such cases the personal healing experience of the therapist as well the relationship to the client are crucial to the journey.

Most psychotherapists are trained in stage one (containment and understanding) and two (analysis of character) of the process of psychotherapy. However, stage three, as explained here, is attempted less frequently. Moreover, the alignment process is paradoxical: it is both difficult and simple at the same time. It is difficult, if not impossible, to explain what inner awareness or the symbolic nature of the psyche mean to someone who has no experience of this. One cannot simply read about it and claim to understand it. One has to experience and work with it. Yet, once activated it is experienced as simplicity itself—without the complication of the conscious mind.

This chapter has outlined stage three of the psychotherapeutic journey, linking it to Jung's essay the *Transcendent Function*, to Assagioli's vision of psychosynthesis, as well as to some key figures in the transpersonal tradition such as Vaughan and Welwood, illustrating how the use of awareness methods for accessing the unconscious may be used. Particular stress has been laid on the use of inner awareness (the ignition of the healing process), a meditative, experiential focusing technique helping the ego to quieten and recede while contact is made with the deeper psyche. While this is the inner journey of the client, it is clear that the role of the therapist is central, and it is to their relationship we now turn.

CHAPTER THREE

Therapist and client in the deep psyche

The relationship between therapist and client is multilayered, but this chapter wishes to focus on only certain aspects bearing upon the theme of healing and work in the deep psyche. It therefore presumes that much of the early, more reductive work, such as the therapeutic alliance, the analysis of character and family history, possibly the exploration of transference and counter transference, and so forth, has been established. The relationship in the later stages, the alignment to the deep psyche and integration, has special considerations of its own and is rather different from the earlier stages.

It is difficult to heal one's wounds alone. Healing, therefore, often takes place in a dual relationship or within a group. The model used in this chapter is of the psychotherapist and the client in an intense relationship, relatively separated from the outside world, where transformative possibilities are heightened by the nature of their relationship. The healing energy and quality of therapists, vital to the whole journey, require that they should have explored the deeper layers of their own psyche.

The relationship between the therapist and client is boundaried, but by any standards of normal interaction it is an unusual framework. Clients tend to be totally open about all details of their inner world while the therapist may reveal little except the fee structure. This framework is necessary for psychotherapy to work. It is not helpful, generally, for psychotherapists to reveal their personal lives or relate socially to clients. The therapy works best when the concentration is on clients' problems and the therapist is not involved with their personal world outside therapy. Strong demands that the therapist should be more revealing are generally resisted and interpreted. For some clients this can be frustrating since they may require more closeness and sharing than is generally available in therapy. There are many reasons for this framework but I want to discuss the one which is relevant to our theme of healing. This rather neutral framework allows the emergence of the deeper work. Personal complexes, attachments, and transferences have to be constellated, worked with and, where possible, resolved for the deeper work to take place effectively. The therapist who intends to work deeply in the unconscious has a more archetypal role for the client who seeks healing, and this role can be ambiguous. On the one hand, he or she is detached and, on the other, intensely involved: which is to say, detached personally from clients but at the same time intensely involved with their progress. Therapists are not meant personally to substitute for the damaged attachment relationships of the client nor to encourage extra-clinical attachment feelings to themselves. However, many a thorough psychotherapy progresses by working through attachment relationships projected on to the therapist. In some cases it therefore takes considerable skill for therapists not to become entangled in these and to help the client work through them.

However, in the deeper psychological work, events sometimes occur that defy normal boundaries. The underlying reason for this is that the deep psyche can at certain times be a *field* shared with another psyche, not an immediate personal property. To understand this better one may think of many normal human relationships as boundaried, having distinct roles with implicit rules attached. Standard therapy, say stages one (comprehension and containment) and two (analysis of character), is also like this, except the roles of therapist and client, as well as the rules of their relationship, are unusual. However, on closer examination even in so-called normal relationships—like those in the family or indeed any in which intimacy occurs—boundaries between people become blurred: a parent identifies with a child, lovers "merge", friends share their inner worlds, and interdependence develops. In intimate relationships the other becomes part of oneself. The psyche, defined to include its emotional components, is somewhat shared, there is an overlap, a common field. Consider the pain that the death or loss of a loved-one can cause. Many describe it like losing a part of their body as if the lost person were part of themselves.

The more deeply one works in the psyche the more the nature of the interaction changes and the more a certain freedom is required from the rule-bound ego. In the deep psyche normal boundaries do not exist as they do in conscious, formal relationships; nor for that matter do our usual conceptions of space, time, and causality. Nothing one is told can really prepare one properly for this experience. What is one's own individual psyche may no longer be totally clear; identity is not quite what it seems. In close-up work in the deep psyche, boundaries can drop, psyches overlap, and the normal conditions governing inter-psychic relations may temporarily disappear. The analyst should be prepared for many strange events to occur once the unconscious field is activated. These are moments of great opportunity but are also dangerous. This can be thought of as an intense, inter-subjective field (Stolorow, Atwood & Orange, 2002) in which the idea of the isolated mind is better replaced by the concept of psyche as an inter-reactive and shared field experience. This requires a different level of awareness of the therapist. During and after these experiences if transferences arise then the therapist should be prepared to consciously work through them with the client. Strong countertransference reactions may occur also and should not be communicated with the subject unless they are syntonic reactions, and even then it is a matter of judgement whether this communication is helpful. Syntonic countertransference reactions are concordant with the psyche of the client and can be useful for interpretation. Dystonic reactions are not in accord with the client's psyche but belong to the inner world of the therapist and are not useful for communication (Fordham, 1960).

Persistent countertransference reactions should be referred to supervision. The emergence of negative transferences in the client should be paid careful attention and repetition of deeper work should be postponed until the negativity is resolved, lightened, or, very possibly, such work should not occur again. A healthy positive transference, but one that does not have excessive idealization, is preferable for the deeper work.

For more rational types of psychotherapy, however, work does not take place in the deep psyche as understood here. Nevertheless many different therapies do well for their clients. There is a great amount of good work done by a more "normal" psychotherapeutic relationship between the therapist and client. Such qualities as containment, empathy, enthusiasm, warmth, hope, and insight go a long way to helping many people. Different techniques exist for dealing with clients' sufferings. However, some require work at greater depth, their wounds are greater, and their need for healing requires something more from the therapist. It can be very frustrating for a client to require work at this depth but be faced with a therapist who is not providing it. For example, a young man in his twenties went to an intensive psychotherapy. He knew from early on that his therapist did not match him; his demands were too great. He nevertheless stayed a long time and worked through a lot of important material, sufficient for that stage of his life. Some time after he had left he had the following dream:

> I am passing the building where my therapy used to take place and
> can see through the window my old consulting room, in the middle
> of which is a tent. I go inside the room and enter the tent. There is
> a large drop as if down a cliff face. I see a ladder down which I am
> supposed to descend, at the bottom of which is my ex-therapist

who is not holding the ladder very strongly; it is blowing about in a great wind. I decide I can't go down the ladder and instead proceed to climb down the cliff in my own way. By this method I feel a lot safer.

This young man never felt quite safe with his therapist; the ladder of the descent into the deep psyche was not secure. In fact, he did not want a ladder (the structure outlined by the particular school the therapist belonged to) for the descent. Rather he had to find his own unique way. In this case, it is not difficult to see that the therapist could not provide the right grounding and healing input for the descent to take place and root problems to be tackled. The client never quite felt understood in the deeper exploration. Therefore, he could never open up sufficiently and the progress of the therapy was blocked by feelings of anger and resentment. These in turn were interpreted by the therapist as projections of the client's dissatisfaction with his own mother; perfectly true, as he was to admit, but this was only half the story. The other half was that this client had to be met in the deep psyche in order for healing to take place. Jung comments on such a phenomenon:

> The great healing factor in psychotherapy is the doctor's personality, which is something not given at the start; it represents his performance at the highest and not a doctrinaire blueprint ... one could as little catch the psyche in a theory as one could catch the world.

> (CW, Vol. 16, para. 198)

By "personality" Jung, at this point, means the therapist's connection to the Self. Jung not only differed from Freud on his view of the psyche and the functioning of the unconscious but also on the nature of the relationship between therapist and client. Their differences on this point are at the root of diverging traditions with respect to therapeutic style and relationship. Jung's distinction between the analytic and synthetic stages of psychotherapy (equivalent to the early and later stages of the model used here) characterised the Freudian style as primarily analytic and reductive, while the style to which Jung himself evolved, he described as synthetic and transformative. The Freudian style is centred on an analytic stance of the psychotherapist in which interpretation is the chief instrument. When Freudian analysis is intensive (say, three times a week) the conditions for strong transferences develop (the transference neurosis), the understanding and resolution of which constitute the cure of the client. From the Freudian perspective the interpretative independence of the clinician is essential so that the underlying transferences can be constellated and then interpreted. This is not necessarily the case for a Jungian understanding, or indeed for other therapies emphasizing spiritual components of the transformative process. For these, analytic understanding of the origins of neurosis is often insufficient since healing requires something more—a new relationship to the unconscious. Jung writes:

> Freud emphasises the aetiology of the case, and assumes that once the causes are brought into consciousness the neurosis will be cured. But more consciousness of the causes does not help ... the task of psychotherapy is to correct the conscious attitude not to go chasing after infantile memories. Naturally you cannot do one without paying attention to the other, but the main emphasis should be on the attitude of the patient.
>
> (CW, Vol. 16, para. 53)

Jung, in the course of Volume 16 of the Collected Works, returns many times to his differences with Freud on this issue. He says clearly:

> Although I originally agreed with Freud that the importance of the transference could hardly be overestimated ... experience has forced me to realize that its importance is relative. The transference is like those medicines which are a panacea for one and pure poison for another.
>
> (CW, Vol. 16, p. 164)

Jung even doubts that the transference occurs all the time:

> The great importance of the transference ... led to the assumption that it is indispensable for a cure, that it must be demanded from the patient, so to speak. But a thing like that can no more be demanded than faith .... I personally, am always glad when there is only a mild transference or when it is practically unnoticeable.
>
> (CW, Vol. 16, para. 359)

The later synthetic stage of therapy constellates the transformative possibilities of the client. In order to facilitate this, Jung envisaged a different type of relationship which respected and allowed this potential to emerge. Thus the relationship between therapist and client became less hierarchical, and unfolding potential emerges rather than being subject to reductive interpretation. The couch was no longer used so frequently; the client and therapist sat opposite one another; the therapist became vital to the healing possibility of the client. Indeed Jung is clear that transformation of the therapist is also possible in this process … "Between the doctor and the patient, therefore, there are imponderable factors which bring about a mutual transformation" (CW, Vol. 16, para. 164). Whitmont (1978, pp. 296–310) provides a succinct account of the classic Jungian position on this relationship.

After these initial considerations we shall now consider in more detail the role of the psychotherapist in stage three of the healing process, here termed the alignment to the deep psyche. There are, in my experience, four foci for psychotherapists:

1. To attune to the deep psyche of the client.
2. To help locate and express wounds as fully as possible.
3. To help clarify, challenge, and where possible, clear out the negativity within the psyche of the client.
4. To stimulate natural healing energy and, where required, contribute their own to aid this process within the client.

Attunement to the deep psyche of the client

To be attuned to the deep psyche the therapist must not only be empathic but also be intuitively linked. A feeling of being really understood, appreciated, or seen is a very moving experience for anyone. Most therapists will have experience of this simple intuitive process and will recognise that it usually depends not on knowledge alone but rather on an intense concentration of a feeling/intuitive type, in which the therapist is linked to the latent, unexpressed potential of the client, as in good parenting. Close friends or lovers who are intensely connected can do the same. A similar process of interconnectedness and intuitive attunement is possible in psychotherapy work, especially in stage three outlined above. To illustrate: the client descends into her inner world, perhaps contacting emotional pain in a part of her body; the therapist is also on an inner journey; the client is above all entering her own personal world so she is largely concentrated upon herself; yet she has also some awareness of the therapist, who is, as it were, accompanying her on the journey. He might be experienced like a warm father or mother figure, or simply as a close companion. She is aware of this help, encouragement, and anchor. For the journey to work well there has to be trust and warmth; any negative transferences should hopefully have been dealt with otherwise there arise defences in the inner journey of the client blocking access to the deep psyche. Again, to illustrate the developing interconnectedness, notice at this point that the relationship of the client to the therapist is a model of the relationship to her deeper self; if one is blocked so is the other. The therapist is therefore, at best, an archetype of the Self for the client, since he encourages its access. While the therapist may constellate this archetype in the client he will later relinquish it to become more "human" as she incorporates it for herself. At this stage to talk of boundaries between the client and therapist is not really an accurate description of what is happening. For while it is true that both are still seated in their chairs, that the session lasts a certain amount of time, that fees are paid, and so on, in the inner world profound changes are happening which are facilitating healing: the intermingling of the psyches of client and analyst proceeds at the pace of the integration of the client's own psyche. These dynamics are not easy to describe and can sound completely fanciful, even to many psychologists. This may have been one of the reasons why Jung gave an elaborate, abstruse, and metaphysical metaphor in an attempt to describe this process—that of alchemy. "It may seem strange to the reader that to throw light on the transference I should turn to something so apparently remote as alchemical symbolism" (CW, Vol. 16, p. 165). In the illustrations of the Rosarium, a medieval alchemical text, Jung views a revealing of the workings of the unconscious in general, and this is a far greater question than just the transference:

> The *coniunctio oppositorum* in the guise of Sol and Luna, the royal brother-sister or mother-son pair, occupies such an important place in alchemy that sometimes the entire process takes the form of the *hierosgamos* and its mystic consequences. Everything that the doctor discovers and experiences when analysing the unconscious of his patient coincides in the most remarkable way with the content of these pictures.
>
> (CW, Vol. 16, para. 401)

The asymmetry of the process has been suggested: the client descending into her inner world, with the therapist a companion on this journey. The therapist is not, however, on his personal inner journey or descent. He has entered into his inner world so as to activate his inner awareness on behalf of the client. At this point there is also a synergy, a combining of energy, awareness, concentration, and belief providing the fuel for the journey of the client. Also, this feeling of oneness in the relationship facilitates the sense of wholeness in the psyche of the client. This replicates the ideal parent-child relationship where the dual-unity of mother and child facilitates the feeling of wholeness in the infant. Since many clients seek healing because of damage precisely in these early relationships, there has to be some healing of this wound during the experience of therapy. This healing lies in the relationship between client and therapist as well as within the psyche of the client. In the deep psyche these two areas, the intra-psychic (within one's own psyche) and the inter-psychic (between different psyches), although separate on the surface, are co-evolving and inter-dependent. The progress in the client's inner world is interlinked with the evolving relationship between therapist and client.

Helping locate and express the emotional wounds

Expressing pain and overcoming negative feelings are fundamental to all psychotherapy. However, sometimes, wounds won't undergo catharsis or heal by normal methods. Damage may be too deep or healing may be blocked. One may visualise wounds stored in certain parts of the psyche. Think of an emotional pain or wound that seems to have disappeared but resurfaces later and feels very fresh; it has been stored in the unconscious only to surface again when one is weak, poorly defended, or when a certain trigger for it occurs. Psychotherapy will naturally examine such wounds lying in the unconscious and bring them to consciousness. This very act of awareness generates some healing and even control. However, in the type of work described here, somewhat different methods are tried since the techniques just outlined—expression and catharsis—may have limited results. The client may say, "Well, I understand this pain and suffering, but I still suffer it".

Location of the emotional wound is very useful for deeper work. The way outlined here is to locate it in the body since, in my experience, all emotion is experienced there. Locating it inside of one's mind, thinking about it, has its limits. It's fine to begin with but it won't get healed there. Experiencing the location of the wound inside a particular part of the body (or imaginal body, better termed) is more fruitful because it directs the awareness of the sufferer to the deep psyche and away from the conscious mind, which is usually part of the problem anyway. It is important to encourage the expression of the emotion in this wound directly. In this process, the special awareness generated is capable of receiving information directly from the wound, which begins to express itself powerfully. In the case study of Michael (above), as soon as he was able to contact and express authentically his emotional pain (the child lost in a strange land) he was able to develop (dream of saving the boy) and progress (change his life).

Dealing with negativity

Dealing with negativity is vital for progress. This mobilisation of inner awareness, and the descent, may also provide information about the attitude of the client to her own wound and suffering. The inner awareness receives information already existing in the deep psyche. It is not deducing information or diagnosing it, an analytic style belonging to normal awareness. It might receive information that the subject is self-pitying and adopts a victim attitude which is totally unhelpful to the healing process; or how the subject resists the healing process within herself. Deeper processes in the psyche are concerned with the client's own negative attitude towards herself. It is not necessarily the analyst alone who points to the client's negativity, it is the deep psyche of the client also. The attitude of clients to their own wounds and suffering is therefore critical. As an extreme case consider those in total denial of their wounds or vulnerability. Such an attitude is not helpful for the healing process since not even the first stage of achieving awareness can be reached. Clearly an attitude of denial maintains the condition. More difficult to see, however, is that even in cases of trauma which have been externally inflicted, when the client was too young to have any conceivable involvement with its infliction, when all clinical and even common sense says she was a victim, nevertheless the inner attitude and defences, erected unconsciously at an early age, become a key part of the later suffering. These defences are self-erected and it is only the subject who can dismantle them.

Stimulating healing energy

The classic psychoanalytic stance is one of distance, the anonymous analyst who interprets from afar. Within this position some psychotherapists barely speak or express emotion. The context of this is a classical medical model, the role of the analyst is mainly interpretative, and there is a considerable gulf between therapist and client (or doctor and patient). However, the model outlined here has a different dynamic. Here, the healing awareness and energy of the therapist plays a vital role in the healing of the client. This applies to all aspects of this energy: the empathy, the concentrated intuition, the ability to listen for years if necessary, the strength of alliance, the belief, enthusiasm, dedication, and commitment. It is of great importance that therapists have undergone considerable healing themselves so that they know the terrain. They do not have to know the exact situation or to have passed through an identical path. However, if they have not experienced healing themselves, they cannot be convinced of its probability in their clients. It is important their healing energy is strong. From this viewpoint the therapist role goes far beyond knowledge or interpretation and extends into personal experience of healing and from there to the relationship with the client.

Therapists can stimulate the healing energy of clients in various ways: their belief and commitment to it are obviously important; they are alert to signs of it which clients might not recognise or value; they may spot it and then bring it to attention; they remember it on clients' behalf; they help look for it in the darkness of complexes and suffering; they encourage clients to go the extra distance; they have knowledge of despair and darkness and can see beyond them; see also how necessary it is that clients pass through these stages, including dark times with the therapist personally; clients may doubt the therapist's ability or belief and may have negative projections, and the therapists' knowledge of the dynamics of therapy helps to withstand these attacks. Therapists should know ways of helping to dismantle the power and dominance of the ego, hopefully having done it many times themselves. Therapists, to speak metaphorically, have experience of working with darkness and light: they are therefore able to help the client work through darkness and encourage the light of awareness and healing to emerge naturally within them. This healing energy of the therapist is a connection to the collective unconscious, the archetypal realm, lying within each individual.

This relationship between therapist and client in the later stages of therapy, when spiritual and transformative potential is possible, may be termed an inter-subjective field. This concept is distinct from those of transference and countertransference. It is designed to explain a key feature of the work outlined here and describes the field shared by the therapist and client at a deep level. The therapist's energy, faith, and good will are picked up by the client who can thus bond positively, frequently, though not always, projecting on to the therapist healthy expectations. In particular, the archetype of the healer can be projected and this facilitates the emergence within clients of their own healing energies. If the therapist does not match these projections this may lead to disappointment and a failure of the therapy. The healing core of the therapist is therefore vital for the journey of clients, who are undertaking what could be the most important inner journey of their lives, not with a text book but with a real person. It is the therapist's inner quality, the connection to the Self that really matters to their journey. There will be times when the therapist runs out of ideas and has to dig deep into the Self to meet the client. These moments are often key in the therapy, where the Self of the therapist meets the hopes of the client. At these times it is no use hiding behind anonymity or interpreting negative transferences; one has to engage with the fuller being, the stage one has personally reached towards one's own integration of the deep psyche and consciousness. It necessarily involves arational, symbolic functions, possibly in opposition to the conscious formulations of the ego. There follow three examples.

Case study. Maria: the giving up of control

A thirty-five-year-old medical doctor, Maria, had been in therapy with me for three years. Her early childhood had been analysed, her character structure was well known. She was exceptionally intelligent, gifted, and sensitive, yet very unhappy. She was also extremely rational; her mind controlled everything including most of the therapy. One night she had the strangest dream that in deepest Mongolia there was a shaman who held a doll in his hand. This doll was herself, her spirit image as it were. The shaman held the doll closer to the fire and looked into her eyes. Maria woke up in great anxiety lest this doll be lost. Her last dream memory was of dogs around the camp fire snarling.

In session, Maria began to analyse the dream herself. "Let's see", she pondered as she sat back in the sofa, "what tools can we use to understand this dream? Ah yes, the doll must be myself as a baby and the shaman is my mother who made me suffer so much. And yes, the dogs, umm, they must be my rage at my mother and father for treating me in the way they did". Maria looked at me with painful triumph. Now this was a perfectly respectable interpretation and fully in line with the stories she told of her family life. Intellectually, I might have agreed with her—except I couldn't. I felt a protest rise from the centre of my chest. So we sat in tense silence for a few minutes, allowing the ingredients to "stew", letting the tension build. Me, considering her interpretation on the one hand, but at the same time listening to something within, building up a head of steam; her, waiting in a painful tension trying to appear normal: me, trying to assess how I felt about her assuming control of the interpretation; her, feeling compelled to interpret and control, yet feeling ultimately unhappy with the outcome: me, deciding there was something deeper than the control issue between us and that I needed to listen to this rising force which reacted to the content of her interpretation; her, wondering if her interpretation was all there was to it: me, deciding to let this force express itself somehow, but how?; her, tense and waiting. Me, letting this energy from my chest rise into my throat and express itself quietly … "So, a doll, a shaman and a fire", I say slowly. She realizes I am not accepting her interpretation; her body relaxes and she sinks within herself; she says spontaneously, "Do you think I should go to Mongolia?"

Comments: this part of the session was a turning-point in her therapy. Up to this point, Maria was not given to spontaneous, arational decisions that could disrupt her life and medical career. She was now ready to give up control but this required trusting to the deeper psyche outside of the ego and this depended on her relationship with me, in turn depending on my relationship to the Self. As a matter of fact she did go to Mongolia, she actually did meet a shaman-doctor, she returned, changed her life and her attitude towards her unconscious. She came to believe in the reality of her inner world, how it could be expressed in symbols and how the control by her conscious mind had been damaging her. She found a source of new creativity which was emotional and intuitive; she became a wiser and more mature person and moved to the next stage of her life. She became the fuller human being that lay within her evolving potential. We didn't do much interpretation of this dream in the session or indeed afterwards. It was like a gift one brings into the light rarely, which too much interpretation might diminish; it could do its work best by working arationally in an organic manner within her psyche. Since her tendencies had up to this point been towards the rational and the controlling, it was important for her development that these be displaced in order for her arational energies to emerge. The interpretation of her dream would come about naturally without being forced.

At this turning-point of the session there were many responses available to me which text book training or my "inner supervisor" might suggest. Certainly, a classic interpretation, provided by her as it happened, could have been developed fully in line with Freudian principles, which so often interpret dreams as the elaboration of family dynamics, especially of the early years. Alternatively, I could have concentrated upon the transference and countertransference situation, a method espoused by Kleinians and Freudians alike, for whom such dynamics constitute the crux of the therapeutic interaction and interpretative field. I could have pointed to her need to control the session and her therapist by interpreting the material herself. I could have used my countertransference (my feeling of being controlled by her) to explore this dynamic in more detail: how she feels controlled by her parents; how she in turn tries to control them; how she tries to control her boyfriend; how she hates to lose control but frequently does. Any number of fruitful pathways could have flowed from this by my following a transference/countertransference interpretive line. All these techniques are important parts of the portfolio of the therapist; however at this point I reacted differently because of her dream. Something so arational, symbolic, provocative, and powerful came from her dream, erupting into the session and within me. At this point, both client and therapist are in a suspended tension, strangely and powerfully connected in their deeper psyche, an inter-subjectiveness, outside of their normal consciousness which, on the surface, is following the normal rules of conduct. Underneath, however, things are not normal at all. A spirit, an energy, a strange message, powerful emotions have come from the client's dream world. She tries to interpret and control them; she also tries to control her therapist and the session; but this message from the unconscious is pushing its way to the surface, bubbling, insistent, strange, and compelling. It seemed it had been given to me by the unconscious of the client to try to express its real meaning. After all, if it was left to her then it would be interpreted intellectually and repressed, its vital energy stolen, and it would sink again below the surface of consciousness, to snarl and be angry, to convert into a feeling of fiery rage, then helplessness and depression. The doll (her lost but potential real self) needed to be put into the fire of transformation by the energy of her deep psyche (shamanic energy). This is somebody on the verge of transformation who needed the therapist to meet her not just with interpretation and intellect but with deeper aspects of the psyche, especially those connected with healing and transformative energies. Her emergent self lay in her vast, hidden, up to now empty unconscious—her inner Mongolia.

Case study. John and the persecutory mind

John had been seeing me once a week for a year. He had many problems from his childhood and had discussed these with his previous therapists. Although his understanding of his problems and compulsions was considerable, he remained somehow blocked. His mind was excessively intellectual, his feelings were volcanic and prone to extremes, and he was continually acting out in the outer world his inner paranoid conflicts. Despite possessing considerable knowledge of his emotional damage very little changed in his inner world. Reminders that his excessive mental dominance was unhealthy simply reinforced his desire to understand his problems, but the mechanism of how to change eluded him.

As I was listening during a session I wondered how his mind could be turned off and how his inner world could speak. For ten minutes I went into a slight trance state and began to pay attention to my body, especially the key emotional body centres. I quickly experienced a pain in my stomach, clearly emotional; I paid it more attention and encouraged it to speak. It said "Get me out of here, this is intolerable, I am being crushed, HELP!" I next asked John if he would like to do a scan, quickly explaining the procedure—light meditation, breathing exercise, awareness of body centre and pain, and then allowing this centre to speak. He agreed and we began. After five minutes I asked if he could detect anything in his body. He said no, but I encouraged him to stay there. He mentioned a sensation of vague pressure in his stomach. I encouraged him to focus on the breathing but also to become aware of the centre of pain. During this time I re-experienced the voice—"This is intolerable". We exited the scan after about ten minutes and I enquired about the pressure he had felt. He replied he felt some strange feelings but could not articulate them. I decided to tell him what I had experienced: my trance state, the pain in the stomach, the voice and what it said. I suggested this might not be my voice or complex, but his. I explained that the anxieties he experienced in the world were somehow mirroring his inner conflicts and that a vital part of himself seemed repressed, in trouble, oppressed by his mind and its dominance. This repressed, inner, essential self was finding the pressure intolerable and was being crushed. He found this experience and "interpretation" startling but useful. It served as a milestone in his therapy. This was because it not only clarified things in the short run but also meant he could work with this "knowledge" and integrate it in the longer term.

Comments: such techniques are not recommended for indiscriminate use. It would be ludicrous to believe that whatever one feels or imagines as a therapist must be a useful countertransference. Even when such phantasies are accurate it is not always prudent to share them since this can de-stabilise clients; the usual recommendation is to be more circumspect in the use of countertransference phantasies or feelings and work with them in the coming sessions, keeping them as useful knowledge. However, as the reader will now be aware, this book is for the more unusual therapeutic situation, that which is more typical of a therapy with a spiritual dimension in which healing components of the psyche are activated. The experience described above is possible because of the existence of an inter-subjective field, a sharing of the psyche with another, which is possible when healing intelligence and the deep psyche are activated. It becomes possible for information to be transmitted across the field from one psyche to another which may be subconscious in the client but constellated in the therapist (other therapists in different healing disciplines, such as Cranialsacro Therapy, experience this also). I do not normally share this information unless I feel the client can use it. However, when I do tell them what I have experienced, on their behalf so to speak, they do not find the process difficult to understand, and appreciate such resonance. Notice however, this is not just another form of empathy but, I argue, an active interchange in the deep psyche. Normally the information and feelings generated are of a surprising quality, unlike empathy where one can imagine how the other person feels based on understandable and normal sharing of emotions.

Case study. Julienne and repressed pain

Julienne, thirty two years old, was a talented young woman who had been seeing me for about a month. She was skilled in contacting her inner world, experiencing her core emotions intensely and directly; she was very capable of symbolic work. Although this book has character-ised a four-part structure to the psychotherapy process, with scanning and healing more typical of the later stages, it should be remembered there are exceptions, especially when certain clients prove very capable of benefitting from such work at the start the therapy. Typically, they have had a spiritual background in yoga, meditation or something similar.

Julienne was prone to paralysing anxiety attacks. Although many were clearly triggered by her external world, she felt they really arose because of something in the inner. In most cases, it is my custom to try a small scan first, something light and quick. I then watch carefully and ask clients questions concerning the experience immediately after the scan in the following session, including whether they found such expe-riences worthwhile and wished to proceed with such methods. If they found them frightening, it may be better to withdraw from these meth-ods and adopt more usual ones. In some cases the phantasy material experienced by the client contains clear images of psychological danger (for example, entering a disused mine which collapses on entering, or a boggy terrain which feels unsafe, or impossible weather conditions making a journey unwise). Since the phantasy world here operates quite similarly to the dream world, the therapist is alert to the mes-sages/omens in the phantasy images.

In my own caseload I have had a number of clients with a spiritual or creative background who find such techniques useful. Thus, the majority of these who experience them for the first time attest to their benefits and often state, without being asked, that they wish to go fur-ther. This may well not be the case for other therapists with dissimilar caseloads.

Julienne's first light scan went well although it threw up intense material. Her dreams were also dramatic and full of symbols of poten-tial change. After her next anxiety attack she told me she was puzzled because she was unclear as to its cause. I asked if she wished to scan the problem and she agreed. We entered quickly into the light trance state and I felt a countertransference pressure in my sternum. I asked her if she felt any sensation or emotion in her body (i.e., her imaginal body) and she pointed to her sternum also. This reassured me the session would be useful since the synergistic co-experience of identical body centres is a good sign of the healing field being activated. After this point I experienced feelings of tears and sadness in my sternum area. We were able to participate in the emerging scan (ten to fifteen minutes in length) in a fruitful dialogue. She proved very capable of contacting her own material, bringing it into awareness and sharing this verbally during the scan.

The calm breathing from the start was very important for this client because of her intense emotionality. My tone of voice, presence, and so on was rather flat and matter of fact so as not to exaggerate the potential storm to come. "And do you feel any emotion, hear any voice, or sense anything within this centre you have contacted?" I ask.

She replies she is unsure so I mention she can ask her inner self, this body centre she has contacted. She does so and says, "I feel furious". This was interesting, although it did not coincide with my counter-transferential feeling of sadness. So I asked her simply to stay with this emotion and also focus on the breathing, a source of calmness.

A few minutes later she says "I feel so, so sad" and weeps profusely. Again, the co-incidence of our emotions across the field is a positive feature. The productive attitude of the therapist is an intense alertness to the transformational possibilities emerging in the client. Over-sympathetic reactions may miss the real opportunity for decisive intervention and change. At this stage, simply the right question can unlock potential.

Risking her being overwhelmed by tears, I suggest she ask her inner self as to the cause of her sadness. She replies she feels so let down by her family and again cries profusely. There follows a period of about five minutes in which she cries but recovers and returns to her focus on the breath. Finally, I ask her inner self about the consequences of her family situation. Her inner self replies "I [i.e., her inner self] was neglected and became very anxious while the rest of me [i.e., her ego personality] became tough and apparently independent".

Although this experience was very revealing and emotional for Julienne, the contents of this scan are typical of many therapy situations in which vulnerable emotion lies beneath the surface of an armoured exterior. Repressed emotion, specifically hysteria, after all, lies at the origins of psychoanalysis. A number of features of the scan are worth noting: it is a container for the experience of intense repressed emotion; it has a clear structure, agreed in advance; it has escape possibilities (clients can "surface" at will); it promotes an activation of inner awareness which has healing properties; it has the real possibility of uncovering deep repressed material much faster than the normal pace of psychotherapy.

In this particular case Julienne also proved very adept at switching the centre of her consciousness. To begin with she had a normal ego-self which agreed to be on standby while activating inner awareness; second, she switched the centre of her consciousness to the body centre in pain and spoke from it in the first person ("I feel this or that", directly from that centre) allowing the complex of emotion a voice and feelings of its own, that is, she treated it as totally real and could become it; third, she could switch easily from her ego self to her inner self back to her ego self, and ask questions of her inner self very quickly; fourth, she could surrender her ego-self temporarily to me and allow me to ask her inner self questions as if I were her ego self; fifth, she found no difficulty in sharing her inner self with a trusted other and, if necessary, allowing me to voice any feelings I had, as if they were hers. Such facility in the activation of different parts of the self—suspending the ego, sharing of the field, and switching from one centre to another yet returning securely to the ego self at the end of the scan—is a very healthy sign. Flexibility of and within the psyche is part of healing intelligence. Such a conclusion may surprise some readers but rigidity of the ego position is not a healthy sign for deep work. The role of the psychotherapist in the healing process is not, therefore, one of distance and anonymity. It is one respecting proper clinical boundaries, but there are important times when there is co-evolution and mixing of psyches at a deep level and healing intelligence is activated, stimulated and shared. It is useful to think of the Self, the inner directing centre of an individual, as having shared-field properties—not a personal possession but a manifestation of the collective unconscious.

Jung's pioneering views in the first half of the twentieth century on the different role of the therapist–client relationship were only partially taken up by his own followers, many of whom remained wedded to a more psychoanalytic approach. However, in the second half of the century it became possible to access an extensive literature on the world's religions and healing traditions such as shamanism, Eastern philosophies, and spiritual practices, which became better known in the West. Spiritual practitioners, healers of all descriptions, became part of the healing/spiritual/psychotherapy industry. Sollod (1993), for example, a clinical psychologist from the United States, summarises a coherent, ancient, but still living, tradition of healing practices and attitudes as they impact on psychotherapy. This tradition includes components such as: the predominance of intuitive and feeling states as opposed to rational and factual ones; the importance of non-ego, trance, altered, or transcendent states of consciousness; the lack of boundary between healer and "healee", and indeed the possibility of temporary fusion states between them; the emphasis on the transformative potential of clients instead of viewing them as sick or limited; the use of common spiritual techniques such as meditation or prayer; the importance of visualization techniques. Psychotherapists who work with a spiritual dimension have increasingly changed the style of interaction with clients and also reconceptualised their practice as information on the variety of healing techniques used throughout history becomes available. We have become aware, for example, that shamanistic techniques, still in use in some parts of the world, are among the most ancient healing and spiritual practices we know of (Taylor, 1985). As practitioners become aware of the long healing traditions they may learn more from them.

Other psychotherapists have, of course, commented on these matters. Vaughan says with respect to the therapist: "in bringing healing awareness to any relationship he or she provides the optimum conditions for the natural self-healing of the psyche to unfold" (Vaughan, 1985, p. 186).

Vaughan describes five levels of healing awareness:

Physical healing awareness, for example positive mental imagery, can be used to battle against physical disease or impairment.

Emotional healing awareness involves the full, honest, direct exploration and expression of all important emotions both positive and negative. Clearly, this is a central goal for almost all psychotherapies.

Mental healing awareness, can concentrate on negative thought patterns and attitudes to facilitate the healing process.

Existential healing awareness—beyond emotions originating in one's personal upbringing there are often deeper emotions to do with existence itself, such as dread, terror, fear of decay, and death which lie at a more universal level of the human psyche aware of its own impermanence. Naturally, healing awareness addresses this area.

Spiritual healing awareness—for Vaughan, just as the ultimate source of all types of love is a universal love so, too, the source of all healing awareness is the transpersonal Self. The healing of the normal egoic self is its transcendence, the ending of the defensive operations of the ego consciousness that splits the world into me and other, my consciousness and the rest of world. Spiritual healing awareness is the highest form.

It follows from Vaughan's exposition that the relationship between psychotherapist and client optimally promotes healing awareness at all these levels (with the probable exception of the first level of physical healing awareness). To her stimulating framework I would add that the relationship between psychotherapist and client in the inter-subjective field, as described in these pages, demonstrates the activation of healing energy when the boundaries between two psyches fall away, that is, the inter-subjective field, the potential inter-connectivity between therapist and client, is in itself a transcendence of the individual egoic self.

Schwartz-Salant describes identical phenomena with his exploration of the subtle body and "interactive field". He suggests that:

> The interactive field can be comprehended only as a third presence, which often takes the form of an unconscious dyad … the imaginal model, which incorporates the alchemical imagery of the coniunctio and its attendant stages.
>
> (Schwartz-Salant, 1989, p. 160)

Whitmont describes this peculiar and intense stage of interconnectivity and its crucial contribution to the healing process thus:

> Purely "technically" the most effective treatment is when the healer steps back from his ego needs, expectations and projections, pet theories, medicines and viewpoints. Thus in an "altered state of consciousness" having renounced potentially contaminating ego

needs, the healer experiences and observes the patient's state from "within" as though in a conscious and temporarily empathic merger.

(Whitmont, 1993, p. 200)

Rowan (1993), in a very wide-ranging and informative book on the transpersonal in psychotherapy, has a chapter on "Linking and Alchemy". The term "linking" parallels the concept used here of the inter-subjective field. Rowan usefully distinguishes it from the concepts of empathy, identification, and countertransference, likening it to Stanislav Grof's (1988) terms "dual union" and "identification with other persons" involving a "loosening or melting of the boundaries of the ego" in the relationship between client and therapist. Other therapists, whose ideas on this topic are outlined by Rowan, include Alvin Mahrer's (1996) "experiential listening" and "complete sharing of the client's phenomenal world"; van Deurzen's (2002) "merging of two beings"; Samuels' (1989) "embodied countertransference"; Schwarzt-Salent & Stein's (1984) "subtle body" and "imaginal reality"; Field's (1996) fourth dimension—the "simultaneous union and separation of self and others"; Bion's updating of John Keats' idea of Negative Capability (Symington & Symington 1996); Sterling & Bugental's (1993) "collapse of separated consciousness into one melded experience"; and many more. Clearly this is not just an alternative or strange idea. Rowan makes it abundantly clear that it has been commented on, observed, and explored by many prominent therapists across a range of schools. Indeed for some therapists it is not just an occasional experience but something that can be taught in workshops and embodied in training.

Synergistic co-experience in the inter-subjective field

The ability to contact the deeper layers of the psyche is, then, of great benefit to the healing process. The resonance of the therapist, his/her knowledge of the healing field, helps the client in this experience. It is argued in this chapter that there may emerge some usual features once the inter-subjective field is constellated. A field is an area of influence and a shared field is where two psyches, apparently separate, have temporarily dropped their boundaries, and a non-verbal sharing of experience, often in the form of images, takes place. This is a manifestation of healing, not belonging to an individual psyche; it is the intelligence that organises the field itself. Synergistic possibilities, the joint potential of the deep psyche of both therapist and client, are potentially constellated, thus augmenting the healing experience.

It is normal in depth psychotherapy to talk of the importance of empathy, intuition, and countertransference. However, here it is the quality of resonance of the therapist that is the key. This requires that therapists quieten their minds and align to the healing intelligence of the field between them and their clients. In the work described here, they may resonate in their imaginal bodies to the distress, complexes, and also healing potential within the psyche of the client. They may pick up images (sometimes feelings, voices, and even sounds) which are symbols of the client's suffering and healing intentionality. Different levels of resonance are possible:

Resonance at distance

This describes the client entering the deeper psyche, say in a scan, constellating a question or a problem, engaging with the deeper psyche while the therapist is not participating in the client's descent and not receiving any images.

Resonance through inter-reaction

Here the client may communicate with the therapist during the experience, thus allowing the possibility of participation, perhaps a question or suggestion. The case study of Patricia (above) showed in the early part of the scan some communication between us, leading to a suggestion which moved the process forward.

Empathic resonance

Here the therapist has entered into the descent and picks up images or symbols that closely parallel the inner experience of the client in a general way. For example:

> Susan comes to therapy with a dream of a horse that has been injured. Instead of giving an interpretation of the dream, she is encouraged to seek the meaning within herself. She closes her eyes, breathes calmly, enters a meditative state, then focuses on the area of her body (in this case her solar plexus) where she feels this horse

image to be. In her inner world she returns to childhood, a period in which she loved horses and used to go riding with her father. As a teenager her love became confused, she became distant and turned away from him. During this scan she becomes aware that the love for her father is buried within her and without it her sense of identity has become lost. She behaves as if she is injured. The therapist meanwhile, in close resonance, feels her distress and confusion in his own chest yet becomes aware of a warmer feeling in the heart.

Comments: here we observe a general resonance, responding empathically in the deep psyche with a general similarity of imaging and feelings.

Inter-subjective resonance

Here therapist and client are partially inter-subjectivised: the upper layer of their personalities (ego consciousness) is largely suspended, although more in the client that the therapist; the personal unconscious of the client has brought a complex for exploration and the healing intelligence of the deeper psyche is activated. With respect to the therapist the personal unconscious is not interfering (no personal complexes are activated) and the deeper psyche is activated. The therapist may then receive images that very closely resemble those in the client's deep psyche, with no verbal exchange between them. In some cases the therapist may receive deeper images than the client's and may anticipate the movement of the client's psyche, its healing intentionality or entelechy. Transmission across the field is possible. (Those who want to study this further might look at other healing disciplines, such as Cranial-sacro Therapy, where the interaction between practitioner and client is based on such ideas and practices (Sills, 2001, Ch. 6)). In my experience, this inter-subjective resonance is not exactly two-way since the client and the therapist are concentrating on the resolution of the client's own suffering, not the therapist's. The therapist is therefore attuned to the client's personal unconscious, not the other way around. The following case study gives a flavour of how this works.

Case study. John

John was in therapy for three months before he tried this type of inner work using scans. He is concerned that he might never be able to love his girlfriend since he has been unable to get over the loss of his first love. He feels damaged and points to his heart. In his scan I have rapid access to first, painful feelings in my heart and second, to a number of images. The first of these is a pump, under pressure, on the floor of a ship and I wonder if it will do the job of clearing the water. The second is of a young child in a nursery who is crying for his mother. John did not communicate verbally in the scan but in the subsequent debriefing he told me that he had a direct image of his heart and that it was beating irregularly and seemed to be suffering. He is concerned to know the origin of the problem. He next had an image of himself talking to his mother but then of her fading away in the distance leaving him in pain.

Comments: here we observe the close similarity of the series of images in therapist and client (pumps, hearts, pressure, suffering, mother, etc.). The symbols seem to constellate across the field synchronistically. In this case we have the additional information, not known to myself before, and not properly registered by John, that he had an early attachment problem with his mother, deeply influencing his feelings and, indeed, his capacity to love.

In summary, the connection of therapists to their own healing intelligence is of great benefit to clients' progress. Four foci have been suggested for the psychotherapist at this stage, characterised as the alignment of the consciousness to the unconscious of the client. These are first, to help the client attune to the unconscious—the more the therapist is attuned then the easier it is for the client to find a way of being so; second, to help the client express complexes and emotional pain; third, to help clear out negative attitudes, such as self-pity or depressive tendencies impeding clear access to the deeper material; fourth, to help locate the healing energy lying in the psyche of the client, and for this the quality and resonance of the healing energy of the therapist is crucial. Finally, there is no progress without the therapist's personal experience of these healing methods. They cannot be simply read and applied. Moreover, while the wounded-healer is a common metaphor in the healing professions this should not be used by practitioners as an excuse for avoiding the reality of their own wounds and assessing the state of their own healing.

CHAPTER FOUR

Integration of consciousness with deep psyche

Previous chapters have outlined a four-stage structure of psychotherapy within which healing takes place: comprehension/containment, analysis of character, synthesis (alignment to the deep psyche), and integration of consciousness with the deep psyche. All stages are necessary for the complete journey. For instance, no matter how powerful the experience of stage three (the meeting with the deep psyche) all can be lost without the integrative processes of character reform and a realignment of the ego characterising stage four. Jung, stressing the importance of using phantasy material in order to access the unconscious, writes:

> The meaning and value of these fantasies are revealed only through their integration into the personality as a whole—that is to say, at the moment one is confronted not only with what they mean but also with their moral demands.

> (CW, Vol. 8, p. 68)

By moral demands Jung meant requirements from the Self that the ego/personality should readjust. He finishes *The Transcendent Function* stressing the importance and difficulty of this integration process:

> Consciousness is continually widened through the confrontation with the previously unconscious contents, or—to be more accurate—could be widened if it took the trouble to integrate them. That is naturally not always the case. Even if there is sufficient intelligence to understand the procedure, there may be a lack of courage and self confidence, or one is too lazy, mentally and morally, or too cowardly to make an effort.

> (CW, Vol. 8, para. 193)

Balint (1968) attributes difficulties of integration to a failure of adequate maternal response to the infant's needs, promoting a split between a true self and a false self. The psyche is dominated by extreme feelings, which are not moderated or integrated into the broader psyche. This early deprivation causes a later experience of something essential missing inside—the feeling of some "basic fault" in the personality.

Clearly, there are character components such as belief, trust, determination, and courage aiding this integration process, very influenced by the early mothering experience. Integration, as a practical process in psychotherapy, consists of three parts:

1. Assessment of the suitability of the material arising from the unconscious.
2. Working psychologically with the unconscious.
3. Movement towards a new centre of personality and identity.

Using this tripartite structure facilitates an appreciation of its different parts. It is tempting to think of an inability to integrate as stemming from a single cause. However, examples will show there are numerous ways in which the integration process can malfunction or be impeded, thus derailing the full healing process. Therapists benefit from understanding each of the component parts of integration, thereby enabling more effective interventions.

Each of the above stages will be examined in turn and illustrated with case studies in order that this elusive, often neglected, but central concept of integration may be understood.

Assessment of the suitability of the material arising from the unconscious

Not all the psychological material accessed from the unconscious, be it from the dream world, free associations, visionary experiences, or meditative states, is suitable for integration. Psychotic and borderline material, for instance, can be too distorted and disturbing for the client. In these cases it is clinically unwise to assume it is only ego functions that are damaged and the otherwise healthy material from the unconscious is simply flooding through. Rather the contents of the unconscious—emotions, basic perceptions, and sense of trust—are fractured, split, and distorted. The emotional foundations themselves can be damaged, especially considering that in infantile trauma much of the damage occurs before an ego was formed and while the early self was in formation. Therefore the ego, erected upon these foundations, is also impaired. It follows that psychotherapy, in such instances, cannot rely upon access to and integration of material from the unconscious. It is unwise to believe, in these cases, that some inner guidance is sure to follow from depth exploration. This inner guidance and useful material becomes accessible to consciousness and integration only when the unconscious is in a more healthy state and its healing energies are relatively intact.

Case study. Primary defences

John was severely traumatised as a baby and subsequently grew up in cruel circumstances. At the earliest opportunity he left home, married and had children. Problems with his parents-in-law emerged with intensity and his borderline condition simply added fuel to the flames. Intense "global" reactions (distributed throughout the whole psyche as opposed to being localised), triggered by minor events, would violently take him over. He dreamt the following:

> I escape into the wilderness with my frightened children where I find a hut and take shelter. Within it there appears a spirit that takes my children to an unknown land and leaves me heart-broken.

Comments: the dream can be understood as the emergence of a primary defence of splitting. John found his parents-in-law intolerable and any time they resembled his abusive parents he would be provoked into either rage attacks or flight. In this dream he is in flight from the demonic images projected on to them. He flees with his children, who symbolise the innocent but damaged parts of his own self, which he tries to protect from further abuse. In his flight and terror, an unknown spirit (his primal defence system) finds the solution by splitting his ego (represented by himself in the dream) from his children (his vulnerable emotions). Since the strategy splits his psyche it prevents any chance of healing, since for this to happen he would have to realize his projections and integrate the vulnerable sides of himself, which proved impossible. Kalsched (1996), in his work on trauma, also identifies primitive defence systems as a type of demonic-spiritual function within the primal psyche which serve to protect but cripple it at the same time. Here there is a spirit-like component of the psyche which engages in a radical protection operation but blocks healing processes of awareness and integration. In cases of severe borderline disorder, trying to access early traumatic material may not be effective or wise and the therapist may be better advised to build up ego strength and promote protective strategies.

Recognition of healthy material from the deep psyche

There are many cases of less damaged people, however, where the material from the unconscious and its healing functions are healthy. With experience, healthy material can be distinguished although this is not easy since the language of the deep psyche is highly symbolic, frequently over-determined, condensed, and enigmatic. For Freud, many features of dreams were over-determined in that they were caused by multiple factors in the dreamer's life, for example, traumas, recent events, wishes, something casually observed, and so on. Many dream images are also combinations of different strands of meaning or reference and therefore are referred to as condensed. So what does such healthy material look like?

Healthy dreams, visionary material, and other expressions of the unconscious often compensate for the general attitude of consciousness, giving an alternative, original, often surprising viewpoint with an overview of the whole situation, especially of the role of the dreamer within these conflicts and difficulties. Healthy, in-depth material frequently insists on putting responsibility back upon the subject; a victim attitude rarely belongs to it. An intensely personal, moral dimension exists in the psyche although it is quite unlike that of religion or law. It can give a surprisingly accurate "diagnosis" of the character and situation of the dreamer and offer incisive advice, often in metaphorical form. It sometimes speaks the language of normal consciousness, though on examination the meaning is multi-layered and symbolic. It possesses wisdom of its own and is often very witty. Dreams and visionary material frequently have a compactness of meaning and highly compressed imagery. They can be highly dramatic, sometimes to the point of the grotesque. The practitioner needs to be aware it is not only the contents of the psyche, but its timbre, humour, compactness, and vitality that indicate its health and healing energies. It is as if there is an inner director who has an unlimited budget, can conjure up any scene and use any cast, all for the purpose of holding a mirror to consciousness and saying: "Look how you really are; this is the state of your psyche." Sometimes, fortunately, it also shows the way forward, resolving the impasse or distortion, frequently by an adjustment of the attitude or character of the dreamer. There is a feeling of wholeness arising from more important dreams, as if in the psyche of the dreamer there is another more fundamental reference point, some other centre, which grasps a far larger reality than the viewpoint of the ego. Sometimes, the meaning of such dreams can take years to unfold and only with the passage of time does it become clearer. It is exactly the same for inner, visionary states described here, which have a language practically identical to the dream world. Their great advantage is they tend to be more compact compared to the abundance of dream material; also the subject's inner awareness, a portion of their consciousness, has engaged with the deep psyche which does not happen in the act of dreaming. The direct introduction of consciousness into the visionary experience gives it a focus and impetus towards meaning and revelation. The union of consciousness and the unconscious, their collaborative communication, is the great union of opposites, the *coniunctio oppositorum*.

The methods described here, such as immersion in the emotional complex, imaginal body work, expressive techniques, the use of inner awareness, meditation, or experiential focusing, are only some examples of accessing the unconscious. I follow both Jung's and Assagioli's preference for a wide range of techniques to be available. This first step of integration—concerning how the practitioner needs to assess the health of the psyche and, in particular, how suitable is the material from the deep psyche—is now followed by an assessment of the client's capacity to work with it.

Working psychologically with the material from the unconscious

Many visionary experiences of the inner world may not fully reach consciousness. A client may go into her inner world, descend into her pain, have visions of great intensity and meaning, receive personal and profound information, surface twenty minutes later, and remember absolutely nothing. If this seems strange, consider how little of the dream world one remembers on wakening; the vast majority of the material in the unconscious is simply lost to consciousness, evaporating in the morning light. Such a forgetting is more typical of the earlier stages of the work. However, it demonstrates the point: deep visionary-type experiences may have little or only temporary impact upon character. At first it may be the task of the therapist to remember the inner experience undergone by the client thereby giving it enduring value. As the work progresses such inner world experiences are retained and owned more clearly by the conscious mind. The material from the unconscious has to be worked with psychologically for progress to occur.

At the opposite extreme are those who are over-connected to their spiritual life. They may remember many dreams, keep voluminous diaries of the inner world, be completely absorbed in their own phantasy or aesthetic world; they may see synchronistic signs in tiny details of their life and chance occurrences; they may flood conversations with spiritual references and only feel alive when in the company of other spiritually minded people. Such people, unlike the example above, seem to remember a great deal from the unconscious and can build spiritual mountains out of apparent molehills; they may live only to see the spiritual teacher who is the source of life and meaning. If the first case was of someone not in contact with the inner world, this is someone with insufficient distance from it, a relatively undifferentiated ego, a sense of identity that cannot achieve its relative autonomy but is continually circling around the larger orbit of the spiritual teacher or message. For this person a greater autonomy and strengthening of the ego is required, with less flooding by archetypal material. A critical distance of the ego is beneficial in order for psychological work to take place.

A number of cases now illustrate different abilities to work psychologically. Each case will show how this ability, or lack of it, influences the capacity for integration without which progress, be it psychotherapeutic or spiritual, is not possible.

Case Studies. Different capacities to work psychologically

A woman in her forties, Sarah, came to therapy with depression. She had an intense spiritual disposition and was given to dramatic inner visions. Here is one:

> I am in great suffering almost dying in my mother's womb. Next
> I am in a dark cloud, as a child, bereft of my father's love. Just as I
> am giving up I see a white light that gives me hope.

In this vision of her personal condition, she realized she was endangered from the start of her life, and had been unable to receive desperately wanted love from her father, never having found it with her mother. Yet, she found a spiritual light, a mystical connection which sustained her. Within this visionary experience she comprehended how much pressure she put on people in personal and especially intimate relationships, how much she depended on her friendships, and how disappointed she felt by being let down. This helped her adapt and be more tolerant. Sarah also realized that her mystical tendencies compensated for the emotional deprivation of her infancy. Here, personal development occurs as a result of her visionary experience and the capacity to work psychologically with the material from the unconscious.

With respect to the content of these experiences it is remarkable how many visions are of this nature. They may have a dramatic and fantastic scene, similar to dreams, in which one of the central actors is the subject herself. Information is somehow transmitted during this vision, much as it can be in dreams. The subject will say words to the effect "I was informed", "I was given to understand", or "It was communicated to me", and there follows important information which is highly accurate as to the subject's character state and present situation. It sometimes contains condensed advice as to what to do next and how to progress. This compressed information can be enormous while the images or phrases communicating it may be sparse, rather like a short email with a large attachment. This wisdom comes from the deep psyche and few doubt it when they receive it. So it follows there is some source within the healthy psyche which pushes for personal development, is highly aware of the difficulties being encountered by the ego as well as the psyche as a whole, portraying the state of conflict in all its complexities in a marvellous, compact story from the inner world.

In contrast to Sarah, consider Mathew who was given to inner visions, chakra work, and powerful dreams not grounded in psychological work. In a spiritual meeting he experienced the power of his inner world which radiated energy. He felt he had great insight and had developed a preaching style of conversation, telling others what they should do with their lives. Here is someone possessed by the force of his inner world. There was very little personal identity or ego left. It was impossible to talk directly to him of these visions without a torrent of elevated speech. Fortunately Mathew was not psychotic. He realized, with help, he should leave this inner force aside and concentrate on more mundane tasks such as his family and job. There was simply no psychological capacity, at this stage, for integrating his experiences and achieving some balance between his deeper self and his ego. Moreover, the experiences were of such intensity and power they were dangerously destabilizing to his ego and had very little psychological material in them. He needed to develop a stronger ego, and also moderate the intensity of his inner world before effective psychological work on it could be done. On the ego-Self axis he had no transcendent function or intermediary position and was instead identified with the pole of the Self.

Consider another case. Steven felt cut off from his emotions and was very isolated; he believed he was depressed because he was far from enlightenment and he continually strove for spiritual growth. His depression was compensated by projections onto the guru who held Steven together, giving him meaning, hope, a feeling of love and connection. Steven had a series of dreams in which his guru appeared in a bad light. Any suggestion they were a compensation for his conscious position, an inner attempt to correct his excessively idealistic attitude, was rejected by him. Instead, he offered his own explanation, twisting and turning the symbolisms to suit an inter-pretation favourable to his spiritual stance. Stephen did not have an accessible inner voice or essential inner awareness with which to enquire within himself about his depressed condition. If he had, he might have been able to accept information as to his one-sided obsession with the spiritual path. Instead of a capacity for inner awareness he had a monitor checking everything he did and dis-missed anything out of line with the prevailing spiritual orthodoxy his ego espoused.

Comments: in the above cases the possibility of progress and integra-tion is determined by the presence or absence of the ability to work psychologically. Sarah showed a capacity to work productively on the material coming from the deep psyche, Mathew had an ego which was overwhelmed by the force of his deeper material, and Steven was blocked from access to deeper feelings, replacing them instead with the views of his spiritual group. The task of the practitioner at this stage, therefore, is to assess the psychological attitude and the ability to genuinely work with the contents of the psyche that are brought forward. In two of the above cases there is an absence of the ability to work psychologically with material from the deep psyche. This limits or prevents integration and therefore the practitioner should concentrate on building up this capacity before expecting progress.

The favourable psychological attitude

An unfavourable psychological attitude thus prevents the process of integration even beginning. So what, then, is a favourable psychological attitude? Eight points are mentioned below: the closer to the eighth, the more developed this attitude is. Of course, one does not expect expertise in all these areas. But I suggest that some facility, openness, or at least willingness to learn in the first six areas constitutes a basic psychological attitude suitable for psychological growth, while progress in the last two constitutes higher level functioning and operates when the symbolic, archetypal, or transpersonal world is contacted and deep healing takes place. When somebody is lacking in a number of these, or has them to a limited extent, it is more useful to attempt to develop them rather than expect an integration process to happen automatically. In many cases it is a balanced position with respect to these psychological attitudes that is desirable for effective work.

First, *the capacity for introspection*. A capacity to look inwards is essential for psychotherapy to be effective otherwise there can be no character examination or change. The therapist has the task of fostering and developing this attitude in the client not only at the start of therapy but also during it. Introspection, despite appearances to the contrary, is not easy. Even the dream world, which concerns principally the inner world, at first glance seems to be largely concerned with stories and people from the outer world. For example, dreams of one's children being lost or in danger are common; great emotion usually occurs and a desire to rescue the children is strong. These may occur when the dreamer's children are in no objective danger at all. Rather, they are symbols of something immensely precious in the psyche—such as spontaneity, capacity for play, pleasure, innocence, growth, or the soul—that is endangered. Dreams frequently, though not always, dramatise a story of outer events and people symbolising parts of oneself. The outer story tells the tale of an inner truth. The purpose of psychotherapy is to find this inner truth, for which introspection, clearly, is a prerequisite.

It is tempting to believe that when clients share their intimate feelings they are inevitably talking of their inner world. However, much of this is really about the outer world, other people, family and friends, as they impact upon the subject. Deeper work is more interior than this. For example, a father has an argument with his son after which he feels not only enraged but lonely and self-pitying. He comes to psychotherapy feeling damaged but at the same time hardened. During the session he has a phantasy, quite shocking to him, that he feels betrayed by his mother and shoots her. Our interpretation, worked out jointly, is not a reductive one tracing back some supposed violent feelings to a mother complex. Rather, it is mainly an inner event, of which the mother is a symbol of a quality in himself that he has symbolically murdered, that is, his capacity to love his son, indeed his capacity to love in general—he has become hardened. His inner world is dramatically representing, in symbolic terms, what he is doing to parts of his own psyche: he is destroying his loving capacity. The moral standpoint of the unconscious is to insist on the damage he is doing to himself. It is not primarily concerned with the outer event and whether he should have argued so badly with his son. It is concerned with the inner disposition and the impact on himself of this anger. The above interpretation was "correct" because the father had several on offer in the session and this was the one that made complete sense to him, producing, moreover, dramatic change in his inner world and behaviour. One year later he proved to have held on to this interpretation and could show how fruitful it had been in helping him in his family dynamic. A great deal of the material of the deep psyche concerns not outer events but the functioning of the psyche as a whole. It expresses this in symbols and drama, using events and people from the outside world as its setting, props, and *dramatis personae*.

Second, *the capacity to contact and express emotion*. Psychological wounds, complexes, and suffering, that require healing lie within the emotional structure. Cognitive intelligence, when highly developed, can be an obstacle to emotional exploration since when the conscious mind is dominated by this rational function access to the deeper psyche, in its emotional and spiritual functioning, can be blocked. In these cases the therapist may direct the client away from rational understanding towards emotional engagement. Apart from an overdevelopment of rational functions there is also the blunting or underdevelopment of emotions, which clearly inhibit the ability to contact and express the contents of the deep psyche. The ability to contact and express emotions is simply the single most important platform for deeper work. Without it depth psychotherapy stops in its tracks.

In order to let the deep psyche speak one has to allow metaphors to flourish. The metaphorical approach is a good start to loosening up the psyche so it learns to express its feelings and intuitions. It might begin with the expression of feelings which have to be in metaphor, such as "I feel like I am being *torn* in two", a physical image describing a feeling in the inner world. The ability to use metaphor extensively across the range of the psyche's activities is fundamental to its search for meaning.

Developed metaphor is related to the expressiveness of the psyche and is instrumental to healing intelligence.

Besides contacting and expressing emotions, a further development is to access the truth in them. In order to do this it is necessary that the controlling ego is suspended and a capacity is developed to listen and observe these emotions so they naturally reveal their truth and messages. This faculty is explained (Gendlin, 1981) in an experiential focusing method and was highly correlated with successful outcome in brief therapy.

Third, *to see oneself and others more objectively*. While introspection is necessary it is by no means sufficient for effective psychotherapy. In fact it can be counter-productive when not balanced with some objectivity. The ego can make progress if it sees itself from the viewpoint of trustworthy others. It should stop seeing everything from its own self-interest and, hopefully, it may even empathise with others. An interesting way to get some truth about one's character is to ask an honest, intelligent, reliable friend and then really listen. In addition, the ability to see others more objectively is to lessen one's projections on to them, especially those which are highly distorted and damaging. When projections are withdrawn there is greater self-responsibility, introspective capacity, and ownership of one's emotions. Humility is the start of all proper inner work.

Fourth, *acceptance of self-responsibility*. A healthy psychological attitude accepts responsibility for one's actions and for their effect on others. Suppose someone does not accept that his own character explains a great deal of what happens in his life; he thinks of himself as a victim with no responsibility for what happens to himself; everything bad in his life is the fault of other people. Thus, there is no psychological attitude to work with since there is no self-reflection. An attitude of victimhood is the antithesis of the psychological one.

At the same time an excessive psychological attitude is unhelpful: such as the view that absolutely everything is one's own responsibility; or that one has somehow chosen one's parents no matter how abusive they have been; or a car accident one has suffered was somehow chosen or destined. Attempting to do in-depth work and exploring motives and events in one's life starts from the platform of self responsibility … "The fault, dear Brutus, is not in our stars, but in ourselves, that we are underlings" (Shakespeare. *Julius Caesar*, I, ii, 140–141).

Fifth, *awareness that one's psyche consists of different but inter-related parts*. These are related together ideally in a total system which is self-balancing. However, in practice there are often divergent components which are in opposition to one another and cause disharmony and suffering. Some of the well known psychological implications of this view of the psyche have become incorporated into modern psychological thinking: for example, the very idea of the conscious and the unconscious, the Jungian view of shadow, the concept of projections, defence mechanisms, various complexes, and different psychological functions such as thinking and feeling. Some acquaintance, therefore, with this way of thinking, that the psyche consists of an amalgam of parts, sometimes opposites, is beneficial to psychological work.

Sixth, *the conscious attitude is aligned to the unconscious but is also relatively independent.* This implies that the client is neither cut off from nor over-identified with the deep psyche but is rooted in a healthy dialogue with it. Ideally, there is a creative tension between these two positions: the conscious attitude must be prepared to question the material arising from the unconscious, not all necessarily of a beneficent nature. Darker aspects of the unconscious may emerge. Some of the material can be so powerful that the subject becomes inflated and possessed by its energies and the ideas flowing from it. A certain conscious and critical distance is required for proper reflection. Nevertheless, the ego has to recognise its place in the system of the psyche and be prepared to really listen with humility. In the case studies above, Mathew is an example of someone who is over-identified with contents of the deep psyche while Steven is insufficiently aligned and too remote from them.

Seventh, *the existence of a symbolic attitude.* Symbol, in the Jungian sense, is a representation of something only partially known, since its roots lie in the depths of the unconscious. A symbol has manifold meanings; it is rich, multilayered, and can never be totally pinned down. The greatest symbols are continually reinvented to re-create meaning. The development of the symbolic attitude is at the higher reaches of the psychological attitude and is especially linked to healing since it reaches the unconscious, which expresses itself through symbols, thereby activating healing and transformative intelligence.

Eighth, *the ability to contact the contents of the deep psyche.* Inner awareness, a special inner faculty that is open and unbiased, as in meditation and experiential focusing, is an example of this. It can access the material from the deep psyche and facilitate its integration. It also possesses great healing power. This is not ordinary self-reflection but a very special introspective function, a pure awareness of one's inner world. A high-level psychological attitude is one engaging in such self-reflection in an extremely open manner, willing to encounter new and sometimes surprising aspects of oneself. A narrow belief system, religious dogma, spiritually fixed views, psychologically rigid opinions and theories are very unhelpful since they destroy this open attitude to self-enquiry.

In summary, in a healthy psyche the ego benefits by setting aside its traditional point of view, listening to its deeper psyche and to the views of trustworthy others regarding itself. It advances by accepting responsibility and ceasing, whenever appropriate, to blame others; it benefits by accepting it has unconscious, or at least hidden, emotions which are influencing behaviour; it progresses in self-understanding and self-control by an awareness of its defences and complexes; it is humbled but becomes wiser by accepting its own shadow components; therapeutic progress is enhanced if there is adequate expression and exploration of emotions, while collaborative work with the deep psyche is promoted by a capacity for metaphor and symbol as well the facility of communicating with the deep psyche; the awakening of inner awareness, especially in its pure form, is of great benefit in promoting all aspects of personal knowledge and development.

This capacity to work psychologically, to be tuned in to the way the psyche works, and to collaborate with its expressive potential, is therefore the second major step in the integration process. Without it progress is not possible. The last, critical, difficult stage of the integration process, requiring character reform and a shift in the very centre of the personality, is explored next.

Movement towards a new centre of personality and identity

Healing requires listening to the deep psyche, attuning to its images and communications. There is intelligence in the depth of the psyche which can redirect the conscious self so it realigns itself towards its basic nature and healing functions. Examples have been given of how such information and intelligence is communicated through dreams and inner visions. A temporary suspension of both the ego and analytic processing is required here since, if operative, they block the awareness of the deeper psyche. The analytic stance, typical of the higher functions, may aggressively cancel out the free-flowing, image/metaphor/ symbol-producing deeper psyche. Nevertheless, these more conscious functions, concentrated in the ego, play an important role in the full healing process, for they are vital to the work of integration. Both the ego and deep psyche are required for this process. Healing is rarely an instant matter. It is true the deep psyche is capable of giving information and energy for cure in dreams or visionary material, but it is another matter for the adaption required to be carried out. For this to happen there needs to be a change of character. The reformed ego is essential for the full healing process since it is the subjective centre of consciousness and its personality components.

This is the third step of the integration process and is as important as the previous two. There are cases of those who progress through the first two stages of integration, possessing healthy material from the deep psyche, being able to work psychologically with it, yet who cannot complete the integration process because of the essential requirement for re-formation of character. Here is an example of such a case.

Case study. Beatrice

Beatrice was creative, outwardly strong, and a natural leader. Nevertheless, she was given to frequent collapses in which she suffered a complete loss of energy, lack of any belief in herself, and an incapacity to work or engage in social relationships. After a few sessions of therapy we had identified two causes of this problem: first a bi-polar temperament; second, she had suffered at a young age from an absence of her mother and from a temporary adoption. An insecurity and depression lay within her, covered over by other, apparently stronger features of her personality that were partly genuine character traits and partly compensations for her wound. Beatrice had the following dream:

> I am trying to ascend a mountain and lead a team to the top. I pass by many crevices and dangers. However, I come to an impassable barrier whereupon I collapse in despair, only to find a small goat which is frightened and agitated. I give comfort and it quietens. I wonder about the meaning of this and then hear a voice: "Find the centre and be still".

Comments: dreams frequently produce a dramatic plot or scene to describe the psyche's situation. Beatrice is forever taking on mountainous projects. Having highlighted her restless condition, the dream proceeds to describe her inevitable collapse. However, it also points to the way out of this complex. It presents a scene of the dreamer with a young goat, an innocent and helpless part of herself, like an inner child, describing the condition of this part of Beatrice's personality, her neglected young feelings, up to now repressed by her superwoman protective phantasies. Like a fairy tale, the dream now shows that if she can take care of this part of her inner world she will receive advice which can help resolve her life-long dilemma. If only she can find the way to be still, instead of moving from one project to the next, things will be well. The dreamer is fortunate to have her own inner voice which can present this possibility to her consciousness in such forceful, simple, almost biblical, terms. However, a few years later when Beatrice returned to therapy she was still dreaming comparable dreams. It proved very difficult to change her compulsions despite her realisation of the forces driving her. Realisation is only one early part of the process of integration, typical of step two. Here is a psyche compensating for its wounds by certain defences, energetic projects affirming her identity. Character change proved difficult at this stage of her life. Nevertheless, the material from the unconscious is healthy; it is diagnostically accurate and with a precise prescription; it is also condensed and entertaining—not the symptoms of a defeated or unhealthy psyche.

Successful integration and healthy character components

Integration ultimately implies detailed work of character re-formation, a change in identity structure. This implies greater access to the underlying emotional structure underpinning the ego, which undergoes change thereby stimulating character reform and development. The ego-identity structure does not change unless the underlying emotional structure changes. What begins, and sustains, this change is the power of awareness. Self-reflectivity is the essence of the process. This is the normal but extra-ordinary process of psychotherapy, which seeks, therefore, to reinforce self-awareness by becoming more conscious of the underlying emotional structure, its complexes, difficulties, and healing possibilities. It then helps promote change within this structure. The work of personal development necessitates an intense process of integration which takes time, effort, and considerable courage. Quick solutions are rarely available, especially when the emotional wounds are serious.

In order to observe this process of integration, how lengthy it can be, how it must pass through different stages, how the process advances and then retreats, and how a new centre of personality is formed, let us examine the following case.

Case study. Helen: the capacity to integrate

Helen comes to see me in a state of suffering. Painful emotions have surfaced and are disrupting the functioning of her ego, causing distress, anxiety, and mood swings. Her marriage is in great difficulty since her husband is having an affair. This central relationship, up to now supporting her sense of identity, is fractured. Her emotional foundations, her sense of security, of being wanted, special, and loved have been rocked. Her ego is therefore weakened. She attempts to restore equilibrium by repairing the damage to her relationship. Early in psychotherapy she suspects that her critical attitude has contributed to her marital problem. We explore how she is highly critical of almost everybody. She is now obliged to question her attitude, understand the harm it can do; she may have to empathise with her husband and see how difficult it has been to live with her. Her critical attitude, internalised from her early years, is not going to disappear in the early psychotherapy sessions. Knowledge of her inner world has to develop; clearly this will take time. Awareness of her critical attitude first emerges through stories from her family life. I link it to other stories she has told of being let down by friends, all pointing to the same feature of her personality— her hyper-critical attitude and excessively high standards. She has to think about this, let this point of view settle deeply, otherwise it stays an intellectual hypothesis and no change will occur. She begins to watch herself in her family and social relationships, talk to friends and those in whom she confides to see if they agree that she is over-critical. She returns to the therapy and discusses it further. Integration takes time because layers of the psyche are involved and a challenge to the conscious attitude is posed. The more ingrained the attitude, the deeper the problem and the longer it takes to change.

This process of realising the strength of her attitude and how it influenced her own character and current relationships took months to unfold. Its realisation did effect significant change in her marriage dynamic and this couple came together again. Nevertheless the process of realisation was not accomplished at this first stage; its integration with the rest of her character structure was partial. She might have stopped, for the moment, criticising her husband and immediate family, but when life returned to normal so did she. Her old attitudes, deeply ingrained, regained control. She returns to therapy. The marriage has improved but her critical disposition is still dominant. The difference, now, is she is aware of this feature of her character and somewhere she knows it is a problem; it needs questioning and challenging, yet she is possessed by it. Her integration process has reached a certain stage; it has not penetrated her emotional foundations and therefore has not altered substantially her character structure. Reforming this emotional complex, the whole process of realisation and integration, will take time and involve different stages of the work.

I remind her she can be critical in the interchange in the therapy, sometimes criticising me for not meeting the standards she expects. We revisit the times when this attitude was observed and Helen is encouraged to explore her inner world and, to her surprise, finds an image of her father's face full of anger and fear. She is puzzled and makes family enquiries, learning her father grew up angry with his own father because he was a failure and brought shame to the family. In an effort to eliminate these feelings he brought up his own children with excessive rigour and high standards. He was fearful of failure. She integrated this attitude since she was close to him. She realizes she was also fearful of her father and did not wish to fail him, so she adopted very high standards at school, with her friends, and in the general aspirations of her life—and also with her husband.

This information, with its consequent feelings, took some months to integrate. First, there is the family story itself with its complexity of opposites: feelings of shame and failure, followed by a fear of them, then a defensive response, a determination to apply high standards and not let this failure grip the family again. The critical attitude can be understood as a defensive response which moulds the personality around the hidden core feelings of shame and failure; the shadow of the family is at the foundation of this. Second, there is the relationship between father and daughter and the bringing into consciousness of that component whereby she internalised the values of her father with their emotional components of fear and shame, deeply motivating her father and passed on to the daughter. This came to partly form her character at a young age. It would therefore take time to de-integrate, to loosen from her character structure. Perhaps it would never become detached entirely but it could be opposed by an opposite force within her personality. This begins with the heightening of awareness within her which opposes the unconscious dominance of the old pattern. Integration proceeds, therefore, to the extent she de-integrates the old patterns and integrates new ways of thinking. This process of character reform and change must pass through stages. There is progress and retreat in this process. During this struggle within her, the relationship with me, her therapist, is central, since the working alliance and trust form the platform for the realization and integration process.

Eventually, the work deepens to a pure kind of self-reflectivity. Instead of engaging with other figures in her inner and outer world, such as her father and husband, she begins to look closely at her own self, how it is composed. She has the following series of dreams: first, she loses a kitten on the way to school; second, a child is in danger; third, there is a beautiful man whom she wanted to be with but he was ripped in half by a wild animal.

The interpretation of these dreams came from the growing knowledge of her complexes. The lost kitten symbolises her tender, young feelings which became repressed as she strove towards intellectual and academic advancement. They also represent something alive in her today. The next dream shows a development of the kitten symbol into a young human being who is in danger. This youthful part of herself, symbolising hope, freshness, playfulness, spontaneity, and innocence, is threatened by her critical intellect. The third dream shows in symbolic form not only what happens to her real relationships with men but also what happens to her inner world; it gets split in two by the force of her critical attitude; softer feelings are cut off.

Comments: integration of deep material requires a passage through various levels of awareness and identity structure leading to character change. All of the requirements for the full integration process were present in Helen's case (access to healthy contents of the deep psyche, the capacity to work psychologically, and the ability to reform her character), hence her progress and successful use of therapy. Her capacity for self-reflection and her honesty in facing her inner conflicts were excellent; she proved willing to listen, consider other viewpoints, and question herself; she worked very well with her unconscious and proved capable of grasping her complexes and the forces that drove her; she was capable of expressing her feelings and digging deep into the material of the psyche; her integration capacities were good since all the material emerging from her inner explorations proved of great value; she was capable of gradually changing the role and dominance of character components of her psyche, especially her critical attitude, understanding its roots and origins. Character transformation was therefore evident. The process of integration is therefore arduous but possible within the context of appropriate psychotherapy focused on character reform. The healing of the rift between herself and her husband was possible as she healed the family wound in herself.

Integration and the inability to heal

The following case makes clearer the dynamics operating when there is a serious block to integration, caused by damaged character components of the deep psyche. Therapy is not always successful; the deep psyche is not always accessible and, even when it is, healing is not guaranteed. Transpersonal vision may be possible but the psyche may not have the capacity to integrate its meaning and energy. Sometimes, parts of the emotional structure are damaged and cannot heal, no matter how heroic the efforts. Likewise, for all who undertake this journey, it is important not to underestimate its difficulty. Ironically, in some cases the Self is healthy enough to transmit information of its inability to heal a wound. This can take place in scans, visualizations, dreams, and the like, in fact by any method that contacts the deep psyche. By carefully examining a case where healing does not occur yet where many of the healing prerequisites are in place, one can distinguish and highlight those components which are lacking and therefore, by inference, play a vital role in integration when it is successful.

Case study. James: the limits of resources

James was a forty-four-year-old divorcee. He lived alone and had recently left his work since he could no longer cope with its stress. He had no spiritual background, professing little interest in this area. He had a serious emotional crisis in his infancy and a number of breakdowns in his adult life requiring medication. He presented to therapy with depression and after two years' work he made progress understanding its roots and its impact on his life. He also had demoralising health problems.

His emotional crises had a pattern. He would feel isolated, neglected, and endangered. He would then retire from the world, seeing nobody, simply closing the curtains, becoming immobile and staring into his computer. He would not take care of himself and eventually would fall ill. He would refuse to see a doctor and rapidly deteriorate. We realized this followed a pattern established in infancy. He had been ill shortly after birth and was kept in a special incubator for weeks in relative isolation. On returning to his mother he was passive and required considerable attention before returning to normal feeding.

James could understand the pattern and probable origins of his emotional vulnerability and patterns of defence. This was reinforced by ample dreams, pointing to the origins of his problems and his reactive defences to feeling alone and un-provided for. We could formulate strategies to combat his crisis. However, he was unable to get to its root—a core despair—and heal it. As a result of this stagnation I suggested we examine his deep psyche in a new way to see if any inner orientation could help. James was able to complete the first three stages of the psychotherapy process, as outlined here: he responded to containment and established a good working alliance; he engaged in the analysis of his character and family history; he could align to the deep psyche and access material from it. With respect to the fourth stage—integration—he was able to engage in the first two steps since he had accessible material and he was able to work psychologically with it. It was only in the final part of the integration stage—the requirement for character change—that he faced a tragic difficulty. His answers (obtained in scans) to questions and visualizations, presented below, will provide us, indirectly, with information regarding this. His incapacity to integrate, by engaging in character reform, was the central block to his healing. He requested that I pose questions to him. These questions, although expressed by me, arose organically from the deeper contents of his psyche (dreams and so on).

His first visualization was centred around the question: "What is this force gripping you when you are in crisis?" He closed his eyes and immediately there came the image of himself as a prisoner in a rock cave.

Comments: James was surprised that underneath his passivity there was an immense force gripping him. So, at first, his depression seemed to be something alien and powerful, trapping him against his will and holding him prisoner.

The second question was: "Does the cave do anything else besides entrap you?" James' immediate answer was it also protected him from emotional pain.

Comments: at this point, James could interpret the function of his depression, serving to isolate and numb him from pain and fear. He realized, therefore, he had an illusory feeling of safety since being numb and trapped was a danger to him.

The next question was: "Can the cave be left?" Visualizing himself back in the cave he realizes there is a way out. However, the escape route is very high and he knows he is not strong enough to reach it. Within the visualization he has another set of images; he is taken back to his infancy and being separated from his mother; he is full of tears and feels despair. This ends and he is back inside the cave.

Comments: James hardly needed to interpret this scene. His inner world told him he lacked inner healing resources and energy. He is next "informed", within the visualization, of the origin of this problem. His early separation from his mother left him structurally damaged, lacking trust and belief in himself or in the world. He knew this lay at the root of all his later difficulties.

My next question was: "Can this separation wound be healed?" He immediately imagines becoming a priest in a moving church service provoking feelings of divine love. He is called to the bishop's palace for instructions on entering the priesthood; all would be elevated, holy, and sublime. However, in the next visualization he goes to see the Pope but can't find the way to Rome and ends up in danger on a deserted road in the Pyrenees.

The final question was: "Can the healthy parts of myself predominate?" This time James did not need to go into his inner world. He simply looked at me and said "I know they can't. I just can't believe in them".

Comments: James could not heal his separation wounds in a natural way, for example, by finding love with a partner. Neither could he find this love inside of himself. So the psyche began to look for it from higher sources, the divine. He attempted to unite with this (becoming a priest) and seemed to make some headway, but then lost his way in a fruitless attempt to find the source of it (the Pope in Rome). Here one sees, tragically, the consequences of a lack of access to the higher self. His efforts to heal himself were blocked since he did not have access to his higher self and its transformational energy, especially the energy of spiritual love. Finally, he admitted he could not believe in any rejuvenating energy within himself. Healing energy could not be utilised because of the core despair in James. He simply did not possess character components in his psyche, such as optimism, energetic determination, and self-belief.

James had a number of disadvantages which were hard to overcome. He had experienced early trauma leaving him vulnerable; he was prone to despair when he encountered adversity; he was alone, without work, without a friendship system, and had a history of breakdowns. To his advantage, he was intelligent, introspective, and could contact his inner world very easily; he had an abundance of visualization material which he tapped into effortlessly. Moreover, it was precise in diagnosis, rich in symbol, and accurate in prognosis, indicating healthy components of his psyche. He was courageous since he was willing to try for a long period, through extensive inner journeys, to find the source of his problems and hopefully heal them. He could understand the symbolism of his inner world and visualizations very quickly; however he couldn't integrate the emerging, positive opportunities but would instead slip back into the same hopeless dilemmas. He was dominated by negativity because of his early illness and separation from his mother. He did not have those core feelings of goodness, hope, trust, and confidence. These character components were very weak since they were built on a flawed foundation of early separation experiences—he fundamentally felt despair. In the inner struggle of opposites between light and dark, it was ultimately the negative side that dominated with insufficient hope, goodness, optimism, and self-belief. The two-way positive movement, the flow of healthy energy, between ego character and components of the deep psyche, which should ideally exist, promoting integration and character reform, was damaged. Erikson's (1950) foundational stage of human development—the need to establish basic trust—was flawed. Integration requires the presence of essential character components. In James' case pieces of the jigsaw were missing—progress and transformation were unreachable. However, his deep psyche was healthy enough to tell him that it was not healthy enough to cure him. Various points can be drawn from this.

It is possible for someone to function well in the first three stages of psychotherapy—the early working alliance, character analysis, alignment to the deep psyche—yet falter in the final fourth stage of integration.

The integration stage has been broken down into three sub-parts. It is possible that the first two parts (access to the healthy material and the ability to work psychologically with it) may be highly developed, as in the case of James, but while this is necessary for healing it is not sufficient.

With respect to the third part of the integration process, if, as in the case of James, some inner energy is lacking then healing may be deficient. His visualizations inform us that the origins of this are in his early separation trauma and core feeling of despair. Inner resources or deficiencies may be thought of as character components, which can be positive or negative and are a blend of constitutional and environmental determinants. Strong faith, trust, determination, natural optimism, belief, and self esteem are examples of vital positive components in healing energy.

In summary, access to inner spiritual resources is a precious healing component. However, if inner character components, natural healing energies, are seriously damaged and also access to the higher self is blocked, then healing energy may be ultimately unavailable. Integration is made impossible. This was the case with James, in spite of the rapid access to his inner world, the ampleness of the material, its very revealing diagnostic capacity, and his rapid understanding of symbolic forms of communication. Therefore, in cases such as these, the general healing and individuation process may not be completed. Balint's insight into early damage of the maternal bond, the "basic fault", is relevant.

The Fisher King: wound curable or incurable?

Since the above case study concerns a non-healing wound, despite access to the deep psyche, there comes to mind the tale of an intriguing character in the Arthurian Grail legend, a king with a wound that will not heal. There are many variations of this story and its popularity has persisted, in one form or another, down to modern times, with Wagner's opera *Parsifal* being a notable example. It may have an original Middle Eastern template, giving it an archetypal death and resurrection structure, while its Celtic form shrouds it in legends and fairy tales. Upon this is superimposed a Christian tale of knights, the Grail, chivalry, and the cultural and religious clothing of the European Middle Ages.

By way of synopsis, it tells of a crippled king, living in a remote castle in ancient Britain, who frequently fishes in a lake, hence the

"Fisher King". He has a dreadful wound and his kingdom is a wasteland. The Grail is the cup or dish used at the Last Supper which once held the blood of Christ, the most sacred object for the Knights of the Round Table, the inspiration of their quest and source of ultimate healing. Yet the crippled king, the latest of its keepers, cannot avail himself of its healing powers. Knights such as Percival, Galahad, and Bors try to help cure him. They have to find the remote but wonderful castle, pass through many curious adventures en route, and eventually, after great difficulty, enter the castle where mysterious events take place. Clearly, this castle is in a magical or liminal territory, in psychological terms immersed in the unconscious. In some versions, it is Galahad who cures the King; in others, and more typically, it is Percival, who has to undergo a transformation, a journey of spiritual and personality development from being uncouth and foolish to being a knight worthy of finding the Grail and curing the Fisher King. Percival, on his first visit, fails to help heal him and leaves the castle where he learns the source of his failure: he did not ask the Fisher King one vital question: "Whom does the Grail serve?" He has to return to the castle, an arduous task taking many years, but now asks a different question: "What ails thee?" In some versions the king is healed while in others he dies and Percival inherits the kingdom.

There are many possible interpretations of this story. Those of Jungian persuasion stress the archetypal world. Maria Louise von Franz in the foreword to her joint book with Emma Jung, *The Grail Legend*, writes:

> Like alchemy and its curious symbolic productions, these poetic fantasy creations and their symbolism are also illustrative of deep seated unconscious processes that are still of the greatest significance, for they prepare the way to, and anticipate, the religious problem of modern man.

> (Jung & von Franz, 1998)

This modern religious problem was, for Jung, a loss of soul, here symbolised by the wounded Fisher King. Modern man (perhaps most people) are, like him, wounded and suffering, lacking access to higher healing powers even though the Grail lies within their castle, the psyche. A fresh approach and energy with access to higher powers is required, as is the asking of the right question. In many fairy tales and legends asking the right question, giving the right answer, or choosing the right path have enormous implications. Fairy tales frequently point to fresh energy, wisdom, or solution coming from an unexpected source, perhaps a fool, an animal, a child. In this case, while the fascinating questions are revealed, their answers are withheld, creating suspense in the listener. Whom, indeed, does the Grail serve and what ails the man who has the Grail in his castle but cannot be healed? And why are these questions so important? Here lies a riddle to intrigue any court.

The king symbolises ruling forces of the psyche—the ego and its dominant complexes—that have now failed. His kingdom is a wasteland, signifying that this ruling consciousness has come to a standstill: sterility, emptiness, meaninglessness dominate. His wound is in the thigh or testicles; creativity has gone and it has been called the wound that won't heal because all normal methods have failed. What is required is deep magic and he fishes in the lake of the unconscious. Healing can only be effected from the deep psyche where numinous forces are found. The king cannot do this alone, he needs help, which Percival, innocent and uncourtly, attempts to provide. Yet this sufferer, the Fisher King, also holds the Grail, the integrative wholeness of the psyche unrealized within him.

Such tales may have had great literal significance for those who, indeed, did live in kingdoms where so much depended on the strength, vitality, procreativity, and intelligence (or otherwise) of the ruler. But they also have symbolic significance, relating to the psyche and its dilemmas, its urge to be healed, grow, and resolve the impasses that beset it.

From the perspective of this book, the tale has poignant implications. Consulting rooms of psychotherapists are, of course, full of clients suffering the malaises of our times: depression, narcissism, addiction, abuse, depression, isolation, and a sense of meaninglessness. Emotional wounds often appear chronic and even incurable. Access to the deeper psyche, to the Self and its powerful transformative properties, may be blocked. Each and every individual has a kingdom (the psyche); has wounds and sufferings requiring healing; is required to confront the inner darkness, the sense of sterility, mortality, and meaninglessness; needs access to the higher and original powers of the psyche, the Grail, in order to overcome chronic wounds and allow the kingdom to prosper. The Fisher King is Everyman. The new, fresh, original, innocent, yet determined and long-suffering principle is the Percival symbol, which is capable of transforming the hitherto incurable wound—the division in the psyche and its loss of meaning, its lack of connection to the soul—with its energy, guidance, and transformative powers.

The Grail is the divine inside the psyche and therefore it serves God. In its turn, it is available to all who wish to cure their psyche of its wounds; a blessing, a gift of renewal and rebirth. It is inextricably bound up with suffering. Those who contact it know they must serve it. Everyone who undergoes this path of healing and renewal has to find an individual answer to questions such as these, to find out what is their relationship to this force and intelligence inside of themselves. The Grail is the natural healing intelligence, the wholeness and beauty of the psyche. It is available to all, a servant of none.

Despite the tale being inherently enigmatic and capable of numerous interpretations, it seems it is the Fisher King's attitude, or something in his character structure, that blocks access to the healing properties of the Grail. In James' case, there is also a problem with integration: both have access to the numinous forces of the deep psyche (alignment) and they may be both skilled in interpreting its messages (symbolic capacity). However, James has damage in key character components preventing him from integrating the essential healing energy from the deep psyche and he lacks access to a higher love. These two factors block his integration. So, too, with the Fisher King one suspects some "basic fault" in the integration mechanism, for after all, he has the Grail in his castle but cannot achieve his own healing. It is not that this healing cannot occur but that it requires a transformation of attitude. That is why it is the questions that are so very important; it is the manner in which he approaches the Grail and his own suffering—components of his character have to change. Although he is the Grail keeper, he needs to serve it, to become humble rather than believe he owns it, to adopt the simple (non-intellectual) path like Percival; and most importantly he has to look inwards at what is really ailing him. From this perspective, his inability to integrate the Grail's healing power is due to flaws in his character.

The three steps of integration have now been described and it is clear each forms a necessary link in the total process. If any one of these links is absent or seriously weak the process of integration is likely to stall or fail and the healing process will not be complete. This integration stage does not necessarily have a spiritual dimension to it. In the case of Helen, above, one observes an analysis and integration process with respect to normal character components and attitudes. Conversely when spiritual components of this journey are activated they also need integration in order to become effective. In the case of James, spiritual components emerge in his contact and alignment to the deep psyche (stage three) but he found it impossible to integrate these messages due to some "basic fault".

Integration, therefore, is a multistep process centring on the ability to link and unite healthy and diverse parts of the psyche, especially the conscious and the unconscious, as well as to engage in the concomitant process of character reform, shifting the centre of personality closer to the Self.

The case studies given earlier in the chapter indicate how integration may occur in the therapeutic work and they attempt to detail the process at a micro level—how it works in a nitty-gritty way, how piecemeal gains are made, and what is required for progress. On the other hand, the macro level is concerned with how integration is conceived as an overall process; it has a panoramic view of the purpose of the *opus*, the end goal, the *telos*, the grand purpose of human life, and has been presented by many writers and therapists from Jung onwards. An eloquent and persuasive account is given by Washburn (1994, 1995), where he outlines how the dualism of consciousness and the unconscious is transcended by the integration process—the *coincidencia oppositorum*; how the divisions of mind-body, thought-feeling, logic-creativity, and civilization-instinct are integrated in a whole human being. My purpose has been more humble: to examine at an individual, inner level the components of this process in psychotherapy, how they work dynamically, what may block integration, how the therapist may help, which components of the client's psyche may aid or impede process. In other words, this chapter has attempted to supplement the grander vision of the philosopher or spiritual sage with a practitioner's need to work in the living psyche.

CHAPTER FIVE

Reflections on healing intelligence

The most common answer to the question of how emotional wounds are healed is that it is time that heals. However, this tells us nothing about what does the healing; it simply indicates that healing is an unconscious process, which of course in many cases it is. However, while it is true that, with time, healing intelligence may bring about considerable repair, there are many wounds, simply repressed, which arise again, sometimes many years later, completely fresh. Time does not, therefore, always heal. Others may reply there is a bewildering variety of response to healing. Some people respond very well, others not at all, some resist any healing, others go a long way towards it but falter at some key point. These are accurate observations but it is constructive first to find out which factors promote healing when it does occur and, second, which impede it when it stalls.

It is easily observed how those suffering emotional wounds usually require a human process of interaction to bring about some healing. Considerable reparation may occur if an offender offers sorrow or loving concern to the person he may have offended. Comfort or love from another may assuage an emotional wound. There is a natural repair process in the psyche and, clearly, significant others facilitate this process, especially through loving interaction. The relationship between client and psychotherapist has elements of this. However, there are some wounds that cannot be healed by other people. The parent or the ex-lover who caused the wound may be dead or unavailable. There are even some wounds originating in oneself. All emotional wounds inflicted externally trigger internal defences that can become part of the distortion and suffering of the psyche—that is, part of the wound. Since an external source of healing may not be available, then an internal one now needs to be found. Therefore, once again we arrive back at our original question, except now it is sharpened—what is healing as an inner process? What happens inside the psyche when healing of any sort takes place?

Let us suppose that whatever process happens in the outer world to promote healing, it must stimulate some inner, largely unconscious, process in the inner world that brings it about. The outer circumstances stimulate inner healing, which, because it is so unconscious, usually requires external circumstances and people to promote it. However, once this unconscious process becomes clearer, then we may be able to carry it out in our inner world, independent of receiving love, attention, and concern in the outer. In other words we may begin to comprehend it as an *intra-psychic* as well as an *inter-psychic* process.

Many psychotherapists, myself included, view the psyche in a dual manner: first as a system of interactive parts, sometimes opposing or complementary; and second as having an underlying integrative wholeness. Emotional wounds are usually within certain parts of the psyche, that is, they are localised, rather than being globalised (where complexes or traumas are generalised throughout the whole psyche, frequently immobilising or crippling it). It is a useful technique—and there are many others—to detect these localized wounds in the imaginal body, emotions as they manifest in body centres. Then therapeutic work can proceed. For example, expressive work, direct expression of pain and complexes, may be done, or in cases where this is not possible, then less threatening work, focusing on ego support, may be advisable. In some cases, transformative work may be accomplished by mobilising other areas of the psyche to alleviate or transform the suffering in one part of the psyche. In case this sounds fanciful, consider what happens when one part of the psyche feels anger but is modified or transformed by another part of the psyche which generates forgiveness or compassion—this is the same transformative principle, where one part of the psyche, very distinct from the other, effects some healing. The dynamics just described, and to be elaborated in more detail shortly, are part of the everyday working of the psyche, and they are largely unconscious. In psychotherapy, or other disciplines focused on healing, these may be examined closely. Psychotherapy should be reflective upon its own dynamics, in order that the practitioner can become more conscious, convinced, and skilled in the healing and transformative entelechy. Vaughan (1986 p. 61) makes an interesting three-part distinction between levels of psychotherapy with respect to their focus, be it, first, on contents of consciousness, second, on the process of consciousness, or third, on the context of consciousness. It is the latter that emphasises the relativity of the ordinary self-concept/ego consciousness, instead promoting the context for healing intelligence to function. To make this clearer, imagine someone in psychotherapy who exclusively talks about preoccupations, plans, difficulties, and desires—these are the normal *contents of consciousness* and the therapy will remain at a basic level. Next imagine someone who is capable of looking at the way in which anxiety is formed, its triggers and origins—this is the *process of consciousness* and is clearly at a higher level since it is self-reflective, examining how the psyche works. Finally, imagine someone who can appreciate the very nature of awareness itself, who learns how to activate and mobilise it—this is working with the *context of consciousness*. Such distinctions might form the qualitative differentiation between counselling (dealing with the contents of consciousness), psychodynamic or psychoanalytic psychotherapy (working with the processes of consciousness), and psychotherapy with a spiritual dimension (exploring the *context of consciousness*).

The vitality of healing intelligence determines the capacity of a wounded area to heal itself. This energy may be thought of as *potency* and is determined by nature and nurture, organic and environmental influences. Severe psychiatric conditions, such as the major psychoses, have hereditary components and may compromise this healing potency. Schizophrenia or manic depression can be so destructive that their subject exists in a permanently crippled state. Many practitioners have noted that biological factors underlie many character disorders, while psychoanalysts, especially those with medical training, such as Freud and Winnicott, have stressed how the psyche develops from the body/soma. Indeed, serious *physical* illnesses can impede or prevent the reparative and restorative capacities of the psyche. Healing intelligence may be compromised, diminished, or paralysed if any part of this body-soma platform is damaged. Apart from the biological foundation, environmental nurturing, especially early mothering, is also vital. Strong love and proper care are the foundations of a great deal of the character to come. Healing intelligence, then, can be crippled or impeded by poor environmental nurturing or biological impairment. The opposite is therefore true: a healthy, vital psyche/soma platform allows greater and faster healing.

Haines & Sumner write of Sutherland, the founder of Cranialsacro Therapy who also used the term potency, to describe

> the felt experience of … practitioners of an inherent potential in nature and in the body that organises, animates, and communicates. Sutherland used the image of potency as "liquid light" and the phrase "the fluid within the fluid" to describe his experience of potency. He was very clear that expressions of potency are mediated through the fluids of the body. Other words commonly used alongside potency are tingling, shimmering, light, vibration, electricity, something moving and wind-like. Like the wind in a sail

or the heat of the sun's rays or the falling to earth of an object, we can perceive the effects of potency but its actual nature is illusive.

(Haines and Sumner, 2010)

The potency of healing intelligence therefore manifests itself in numerous ways although the "thing in itself" remains elusive and even unreachable. The perceiving and contacting of this potency is not within the range of normal ego consciousness but requires non-ordinary sensitivities.

Many therapists have noted the contribution of certain character components to the process of psychotherapy. Theodore Reich commented that the primary prerequisite for psychoanalysis was moral courage. Jung also stressed negative moral components of character as detrimental to psychotherapy. But there are numerous character components which actively favour the healing process. Take two outstanding features of healing potency—*expressiveness and receptivity*—both of which are vital for healing intelligence to function well. Expressiveness is the capacity of the psyche, suffering a wound, complex, or trauma to express its pain in a healthy and effective manner. Generally, the more potent this is the better the results for healing. Little healing can be done unless there is expression of the pain and emotion, either to significant others or to oneself. Most emotional pain is in the unconscious; consciousness tends to avoid pain or repress it by one means or another. The bringing of the pain or wound to consciousness is the first step in the healing process but it can, as a rule, be done more easily when it is expressed to another person and then reflected back to oneself for integration into consciousness. For this to happen, as previous arguments and case studies have demonstrated, it is best if the wound express its pain directly and without the impediment of everyday ego consciousness.

Receptivity is the capacity of the wounded psyche to listen and be open. This may be receptivity to criticism or advice from others. But it is also a capacity of the wounded area of the psyche to open, first of all to consciousness. For this opening to happen, there is again the experience of pain, perhaps, for instance, to know and accept that one is wounded, but also that one has caused wounds to others; that one has been betrayed, but also that one has betrayed; that one has been let down or abandoned, but also that one has done likewise. Once this receptivity is increased dramatic results may follow. At higher levels one realizes this dynamic is played out within one's psyche, in an intra-psychic manner: for example, one has abandoned parts of oneself, betrayed one's true self, ignored one's real feelings, adopted a mask and pretended to be someone one isn't—all for what? To avoid pain. Therefore, acknowledgment of this pain is vital to healing and transformation—without it no integration is possible. This new-found expressiveness and receptivity of the psyche is the vitality of healing potency.

Numerous other characteristics are part of this healing intelligence and its potency. These include trust, self belief, flexibility, the ability to meet and withstand emotional pain, determination, the capacity for hard inner work and emotional exploration, to value one's inner world, to be intuitively inclined, to open the heart, to love, to be humble in listening to and engaging with the symbols of the deep psyche. The opposites of some of these character components are notable for the damage they can wreak. Guilt, shame, deep self doubt, and despair are infamous. Character components are formed in the mix of nature and nurture; some seem given from the start of life as hereditary traits; others can clearly be developed by training or conditioning. The culture of psychotherapy has leant towards the belief that love in early infancy is the basis of all positive character development and its lack is the cause of most negativity in the psyche. However, a part of character is constitutionally inbuilt into individuals and is relatively independent of environmental conditioning. Moreover, complexes can "cascade" down generations. In addition, character can also develop through adversity (including the deprivation of love) and wisdom can evolve through suffering. Character components can also be challenged and developed during transformational work.

While healing intelligence is an expression of the wholeness of the psyche, it is intimately bound up with numerous healthy character components, some of which are constitutional, some the result of early conditioning, some the result of training, and others Self-forged. Healing intelligence is integral to the complete functioning of the healthy psyche. It frequently requires the cooperation of consciousness itself, which, when orientated towards healing, is aligned to the deeper psyche, learns from it, but can question it and engage in a healthy dialogue which is transformative for both consciousness and the unconscious.

Healing intelligence, consciousness, and the ego

The ego can be thought of in a dual manner, functionally and experientially. First, it can be understood objectively as a function of mind, providing a sense of planning, control, focus, and concentration by means of testing reality, self control, exercise of will, self-awareness, and executive control of cognition. Repressing and filtering functions, operating with respect to the external and internal world, are required for this. The ego, with its executive functions, selects those aspects of the external environment it decides to focus on, either for its survival or advancement. It therefore filters out those aspects of the external environment which block this process and selectively focuses on those promoting it. Selection/focus therefore is negatively paralleled by filtering/repression. Exactly the same process occurs in the inner world. The ego filters out and represses those elements of the psyche which threaten its stability and seeming equilibrium. Thus painful experiences are repressed, vulnerable aspects of the personality are denied, and so on. The study of the repressive functions of the ego is the core of psychoanalytic theory and practice. Since the inception of the discipline, the understanding of defence mechanisms has remained a most important part of character analysis. The Freudian id-ego-superego construct embodies this model of repression.

Second, the ego, the person I believe myself to be, may be regarded as the centre of one's subjective sense of identity, the experiential sense of coherence that is the centre of personality, attached to which are a host of character components making up a unique character, such as intelligence, diligence, introversion or extroversion, and so on. The ego may believe it owns these character components but it is more accurate to say many are gifts. In the process of psychotherapy these character components play an important role. Some are of great value, such as determination, moral courage, and optimism, while others may prove to be detrimental, such as shame and self-doubt. Some components may need development, such as greater symbolic capacity, introspection, or empathy; others have to be questioned, challenged, and changed. In order for this information to pass from the deeper psyche to consciousness one has to really listen to the messages and challenges arising, and for this the ego, in its functional aspect as centre of focus and concentration of higher cognitive functioning, must recede to allow the messages from the deeper psyche, encoded in another language, to come through. Consider the following:

> A businessman with a punishing work schedule has a recurring dream through the night that a telephone is constantly ringing, but he doesn't pick up. In session he is asked not to analyse this

but simply relax and associate loosely with who might be ringing.
He imagines a friend who has retired to be with his family.

Besides receiving the message, the ego, in the second sense, as a
centre of identity, has to change. It has to let go of the character components causing the problem and allow other aspects of character to
emerge; dominant complexes recede so new forces within the psyche
can emerge. The businessman's principal dilemma of ambition versus
insecurity needs to recede while his more related and feeling side, his
"anima" in Jungian language, needs to emerge in a closer connectedness to his family, also symbolic of his greater self. His deeper psyche
tries constantly to get through to him but he doesn't pick up the message until he stills his anxiety.

At first the ego is involved, in that conscious identity is usually in
crisis or a state of suffering at the start of psychotherapy and the ego is
frequently central to this crisis. A period of understanding the origins
and context of the problem is typical of the next phase. Here the ego is
strongly engaged since it has to question itself. However, for the deep
psyche to be contacted and heard it is necessary that the ego steps aside
and relinquishes dominance, allowing a sense of identity, that which
I think of as "me", to be questioned. Thus the dual aspects of ego, its
functional role as the centre of consciousness and its experiential role
as centre of the sense of identity, are questioned and relativised. As the
grip of the ego is lessened then the subject may listen to the deeper
psyche, begin to attune to its messages, and perceive their adaptive
meaning. Finally, in the integration stage, consciousness and the ego
return to play their very important part since considerable change will
be required of them both. Thus, a healthy dialogue can occur between
consciousness and the deep psyche. The ego, therefore, plays a variable
part throughout: first, admitting, sharing, and assessing the problem;
second, surrendering, dismantling its defence mechanisms and repressive functions so as to allow other parts of the psyche to operate; third,
readjusting itself so character can change. The healing process has, then,
different requirements for the ego at each stage.

The subject of consciousness, to use Jung's acute description, is the
ego. This crystallizes the character components of the psyche into a
sense of identity which undergoes change in the psychotherapy process. Consciousness, of course, is capable of self-reflection, essential to
the psychotherapeutic endeavour. Inner awareness, a rather different

and specific term used frequently in these pages, is a special portion of consciousness, one which is able to look inwards in a non-analytic, open way, uncluttered by regret, aspiration, or duty: it is a meditative-type skill, distinct from analytic self-reflection. However, the activation of this portion of consciousness requires that other parts of consciousness (executive control, cognitive functions, filtering, and repressive functions) temporarily close down. Consciousness is clearly a multi-faceted phenomenon. Its effectiveness partially depends on its extraordinary capacity to select, focus, and marshal other areas of soma and psyche to its ends. Just as in the outer world hunting a prey requires a shutting down of the inner world (one stops day-dreaming) and complete focus for a short, intense period on selective aspects of the outer world (the object, speed, danger, etc), so too in the inner world, the awakening of inner awareness needs the receding of anxiety and desire, plus the suspension of most other aspects of consciousness. Thus, an intense alertness (initially non-focused but later selectively focused) can be the vehicle for impulses, energy, and information to emerge from the deeper psyche.

Transformative healing work requires a change in parts of the personality where the sense of identity resides. This involves various stages in which parts of consciousness are questioned, challenged, and suspended while others come forward to be integrated in a complex unfolding drama of which I will now give a simplified overview.

The client, on entering therapy, is suffering; his sense of identity is usually in crisis. Ideally, the ego is at least prepared to change but is confused. Empathic comprehension is at first applied to the client's problem; this has been described above as stage one—Containment and Understanding. This passes to stage two—Analysis—in which a deeper understanding is sought of the character of the client in the context of the suffering and problems experienced, in particular the understanding of how the client's character has contributed to this suffering. Apart from the initial emotional containment, the emphasis, so far, is on the analytical: consciousness, not the unconscious, has the upper hand. Greater understanding is achieved and consciousness is broadened by this process. However, in many cases this does not bring about sufficient change, and suffering still continues. A deepening of the process is required.

Stage three, termed here the Alignment to the Deep Psyche and called by Jung the synthetic stage, is quite different because the dominance of ego consciousness is replaced by a listening and connecting to the intelligence of the deep psyche. The "elimination of the critical intellect" is the first stage of an *enantiodrama*, in which opposite principles come to the fore, consciousness being increasingly challenged and replaced by an intelligence outside itself. However, as described in the scans in previous chapters, what happens, I suggest, is that a portion of consciousness—inner awareness—is activated and contact is made with parts of the deep psyche where wounds exist. Energy and information are released from these areas as this inner awareness is brought into contact with them. Therefore consciousness, strictly speaking, has been reduced but is never completely absent. Its participation in the transformation process is always vital. It's just that many aspects of consciousness are now in abeyance or suspension (especially the ego and its mechanism of control, defence and repression), so a different form of awareness can be activated, sympathetic to the deeper psyche, which now uses this inner awareness as a vehicle for its expression and change. Consciousness and the deep psyche always require each other in one form of another. They are the *dramatis personae*, the *coniunctio oppositorum*, the Sol and Luna of the transformation process.

The final stage, four—Integration—requires a deepening and broadening of consciousness in response to this ongoing process of alignment, characteristic of stage three. First, consciousness has to be able to work psychologically at increasingly higher levels in order to assimilate and work the material from the deep psyche. Second, ego identity, the centre of conscious personality, has also to undergo change in response to the healing requirements emerging from this process. Thus consciousness is transformed in two aspects (functional and experiential) in its capacity to relate to the deep psyche and in its personality structure.

Despite the above model of how the ego undergoes a process of change and growth, the practitioner needs always to assess the strength or fragility of the ego. Consider the following cases with contrary diagnostic and prognostic implications.

It is possible that the deep psyche is in good condition, undamaged, healthy, but that consciousness, centred in the ego, is out of touch with this underlying reality. In this case, clinically we would say the ego has to change, attitudes need to be challenged, and a reorientation of consciousness is required. Here the ego clearly has to give way, its pride recede; it needs to listen to its deeper reality, to change. In short the ego is the problem.

Yet, consider the case of someone who has suffered deep disturbance at an early stage of life, before the ego could be formed properly. Suffering and wounds are engendered at the foundation of Self and strong defences are formed which try to defend it from further disintegration and pain. The character components of this psyche have elements of damage, for example, the sense of trust is impaired; there may be a lack of belief or hope, a continual feeling of disharmony, conflict, and pain due to early trauma and severe splits in the psyche. Here, the problem clearly lies not in the ego, but rather in the underlying emotional structure. Hence the ego, erected upon this foundation, may also be flawed, malfunction, suffer anxiety and depression, endure dark moods from the deeper self invading consciousness. To recommend, in this case, that the ego should be devalued or disempowered, as if it were causing the problem, is clinically counter-productive and may be dangerous. In the former case the ego has to lessen its dominance and in the latter it has to be strengthened.

In summary, the practitioner needs to be aware of the crucial yet variable importance of the ego and of consciousness at each stage of the transformation process and healing journey and be able to judge whether the ego and its defences need challenge or support. However, it is their challenging and dismantling which leads to healing intelligence being released.

Six ways in which healing intelligence operates in the psyche

Considering healing as an inner process, and presuming the ego and its repressive apparatus of defences, its identification with select aspect of personality, and its filtering/repressive functions have been sufficiently challenged, then the drama of healing may begin. The major ways in which this healing intelligence expresses itself can now be described a little more closely.

First, *wounded areas of the psyche often have the capacity to heal themselves*, especially when these areas are naturally healthy. Someone with a healthy self-esteem, who receives a blow to self-confidence, may recover rapidly; good recovery is a sign of a healthy psyche, that its self-repair mechanisms are intact. This is largely unconscious and is dependent on the natural vitality or healing potency of the psyche. It works best when the psyche is uncomplicated by trauma and when, on the one hand, there are natural positive characteristics such as courage, determination, love, and trust, and on the other, there is an absence of negative features such as guilt, shame, and doubt. When positive features are deficient or negative features dominate then healing intelligence is blocked or compromised and it becomes the task of any healing process, be it a love relationship or a therapy of some kind, to build up the former (positives) and diminish the latter (negatives) so natural healing energy can be released. In psychotherapy, certain techniques facilitate this process, in which location of the wound, self-expression, and receptivity to other parts of the psyche followed by catharsis is very common. The expressiveness and receptivity of the wound area indicate the vitality of healing potency.

Second, *one area of the psyche may help heal another.* One component of the psyche may suffer an emotional wound, which may be expressed in the imaginal body such as the heart area (love feelings) or throat (expressiveness) or stomach (primal security). It may not have the capacity to heal itself, the wound being too deep or chronic. In these cases, another area of the deep psyche may help the healing process. This can be seen dramatically in visualisation techniques whereby the client locates wounds within the imaginal body which are then healed or alleviated by other healthy and strong parts of the psyche. For example, an area of love might heal an area of anger or trauma; or the area of intuition might provide deep insight, helping clear long-standing resentment. In these cases healing depends on two factors: first, the potency of the area of love (which may be lacking in cases where there has been insufficient experience of it in early years) or intuition; and, second, the fluidity and transformative energy *between* different areas of the psyche, for which spiritual practice is beneficial. In depth psychotherapy it is possible to observe these dynamics at close hand. However, similar dynamics take place in the everyday psyche outside of psychotherapy. It is part of its natural functioning. Higher forces in the psyche also have active healing functions. The world's religions abound in stories of healing and miracles of all kinds arising from higher forces in the psyche. Some of the healing miracles, reported in the New Testament, performed by Christ have, from my viewpoint, a tri-partite structure: 1) the urgent request for healing by the sick; 2) the request for faith by Christ—in our terms, a requirement for the suspension of ego and the opening to the numinous; 3) the transmission, sometimes in the form of touch, of transcendent energy to the sufferer. In depth psychotherapy of the type described here, access to these powerful forces may be possible. To use an example from the language of chakras, the sixth chakra can scan the psyche, locate wounds, and promote their healing. It can also inform the ego of what it has to do in order to further this healing process—it is intelligent. In this case, healing intelligence is facilitated by the potency of one area of the psyche and the receptivity of another. Such healing may not be permanent and the wound may still exist, but temporary alleviation of the suffering may prevent the subject from destructively acting out and damaging love relationships.

Third, *partial healing of the psyche takes place as a result of an equilibrium process* by which one healthy part of the psyche counterbalances another area which is wounded. Many wounds are not healed exactly but are compensated for by opposing movement in the psyche, in which case consciousness is changed since the wound or complex, which so frequently dominated it, is counterbalanced by the emergence of another healthy part of the psyche giving an opposing point of view. For instance, one part of the psyche, which has a grip on the ego, holds a negative self-opinion. This may be counterbalanced by another part which has a positive view. This is not direct healing of the wound but some measure of balancing and healing for the psyche as a whole. In addition, the practitioner should be aware that healing of emotional wounds may take place in a temporary manner and that a wound may migrate to different, sometimes unexpected, areas of the psyche thus freeing the original area of its pain. For example, a love wound to the heart chakra can migrate to another chakra. Thus the heart becomes capable of loving again, though the wound or complex may be hidden elsewhere in the psyche.

Fourth, *inner awareness has a vital healing function when it is in union with the deeper psyche.* The linking or integration of the conscious and unconscious is the great union of opposites, and the collaborative harmony of these two areas of the psyche is the major goal of healing and the individuation process. However, consciousness and the unconscious each have many components. A specific component of consciousness— inner awareness—has a special healing impact when it is brought into union with individual parts of the unconscious such as localised wounds or complexes in the psyche. Inner awareness is distinguished as a part of consciousness, operative when the rest of consciousness is in suspension. The activation of this inner awareness is a special catalyst for healing. The ego, when un-awakened to the transformative possibility lying in the deep psyche, tends to block the transformation processes, being frequently identified with cognitive processes, out of touch with the deeper psyche, and speaking a language antithetical to it. Inner awareness, however, does not interpret the wound, whence it came or how it arose; it simply stays with it. This process activates the healing energy within the wound, which needs this vehicle, this specific component of consciousness, in order to express itself. This union of opposites produces a transformative dynamic in the psyche. On the one hand, consciousness is expanded since it is now linked to the deeper psyche. On the other hand, healing intelligence and transformative emotions are released from their confinements in the unconscious.

Fifth, *intelligence within the deep psyche has the capacity to re-orientate consciousness*. The psyche may be distorted and divided when consciousness and the ego are severely out of line with the deeper psyche which has messages and information looking to rebalance the psyche, correct its one-sidedness, obsessions, and complexes. The most obvious example of this is the dream world which can send continuous messages to the dreamer to correct the conscious attitude. Wounds, in order to be healed, usually require consciousness as a vehicle to express themselves—hence catharsis and new understanding. This in itself often requires a change in attitude on the part of consciousness, so it begins to listen and eventually interpret and express the intentionality of the deep psyche. The ego and consciousness thus, ideally, adapt to the healing transmission system and therefore play an indispensable role in its realisation. It is important that ego consciousness retains some critical independence of the deep psyche. A creative dialogue is required, not a complete submission. However, this is not a dialogue of equals since the deep psyche is now accepted as the great originator and container while the ego corrects its illusions of mastery. Washburn (1995) outlines the healing impact of the return of the ego to oneness with the Ground (the unconscious) in later life after a long period of repression since the stage of latency (around age 6):

> The ego here begins to experience the power of the Ground as a redemptive force that heals rather than slays and graces the ego with raptures and ecstasies. As regeneration of the spirit unfolds however, the ego's experience of the power of the Ground is decreasingly negative and increasingly positive ... The integrated stage that commences at this point is therefore one that is both powerfully infused and peacefully composed. It is a stage that transcends all darkness and violence.
>
> (Washburn, 1995, pp. 127–128)

Sixth, *healing intelligence in its most developed form is the activation of the wholeness of the psyche*. To the extent that there is strong interconnectivity between diverse areas of the psyche, and a healthy potency in many parts of it, then there will be a natural vitality and healing potency of the whole, a capacity for self-repair and growth. There are some who feel an incompleteness and lack of wholeness so intensely that it is a wound, a state of suffering, the overcoming of which is the embracing of the natural wholeness of the psyche. This wholeness has elevated and sometimes mystical states or peak experiences which have tremendous healing and reorientation power. The experience of wholeness is the intelligence of the deep psyche which is in union with consciousness. The awareness of the main chakras, for example, as an experience from base to the crown, functioning in harmony, is a wonderful healing experience.

There is a philosophical problem about the origin and operation of healing intelligence that parallels the debate of whether the Self is a specific archetype of order, growth, and integration or the totality of the psyche. The same question applies to healing intelligence: does it come from the Self or is it in the totality of the psyche? There is certain ambivalence in any answer to this or any similar question on the Self. Take, for example, self-reflection and our capacity to track its neurochemistry, that is, the neural correlates of self-reflection. We would expect this neurochemistry to be exclusively located in the frontal lobes, that is, in specifically human parts of the brain. Well, actually, this is only partially the case. The correlates are located in both the frontal lobes (medial prefrontal cortex) but also deep in the limbic (more primitive) system in the posterior cingulate cortex (Johnson et al., 2002). The neural system that serves self-reflection operates in parts of the brain which are widely distanced in evolutionary development. It's as if the deep unconscious and the highly conscious must be linked in order to allow self reflection.

The view expressed in these pages is that healing intelligence, in its full expression, depends on the functioning of the whole psyche: on multiple operating centres in conjunction with the Self. These centres include consciousness (actually, inner awareness), the personal unconscious (actually, the different centres that hold our emotional structures, like chakras), and the collective unconscious (the self and archetypes which underpin and interact with our emotional centres). It follows that healing intelligence operates at different levels.

The primary intelligence is in the Self (Jung), the transpersonal (Vaughan), the dynamic Ground (Washburn), but this is incomplete without the collaboration of the other areas of the psyche and their healing centres. The totality, or greater functioning of healing intelligence, therefore requires the whole (or at least *more* whole) functioning of the psyche.

The metaphors symbolising this process in the world's religions, mythologies, fairy tales, literature, music, and arts are those of light and darkness. Wounds lying in the darkness of the psyche are numerous. Darkness here signifies not only unconsciousness, but especially negativity since wounds usually lie in the unconscious covered with a protective, negative shell. A task of healing in the early stages is location of the wound and penetrative comprehension, that is, penetrating the wound's negativity by comprehension of its defences. Light in the psyche has different sources—for instance, the light of consciousness, a portion of which is the inner awareness just mentioned. There are other sources of light so powerfully described in Tao and chakra practices. This "light" is not simply a metaphor since the subject experiences it as inner reality. More accurately it is a symbol. In chakra terms, for instance, there is a light coming from the sixth chakra. Washburn, remarking on the liberation of the *Ground* after the lifting of primal repression, says ...

> At this transition point, however, because it is liberated from exclusive association with the instincts and it is disburdened of the resistance of the ego, the power of the Ground expresses itself as luminously intelligent and affirmatively outreaching, as conscious light and love. That is, it is able to express itself as spirit ... experienced as pure luminous consciousness, either in the form of a powerful objectless contemplation or in the form of interior fluidic light. Daniel Brown (1986) in his cross cultural study of contemplative experience reports that at a certain stage ... "awareness opens up to the substratum of ordinary perception, namely an incessant flow of light in the stream of awareness" (p. 240). The very energy that normally functions invisibly as the medium of awareness ... here becomes the "object" of awareness, manifesting itself as luminous consciousness.

> (Washburn, 1995, p. 128)

The interplay of dark and light, wounds and healing, consciousness and unconsciousness are central motives of transformation stories. Impediments and resistances to healing intelligence, repair and growth, are also symbolised by darkness, and it is to this subject we now turn.

Obstacles to healing intelligence

There are many impediments to healing, stretching from ignorance of its possibility to outright despair. Below are listed twelve obstacles, but I am sure other practitioners could add more, so common and extensive is this phenomenon.

1. The conscious mind is attached to its repressive apparatus and apparent dominance and control; this is a major block to healing. One of the main tasks of psychotherapy and spiritual experience, intent on deep work, is to Self-dismantle this dominance, that is, to allow the influence of the Self to reshape personality. At this point the ego and its defences weaken and it may become possible for inner feelings and a voice to emerge. The ego has to abdicate, at least temporarily. It is customary for psychotherapists and counsellors, trained in psychoanalytic theory, to believe that repression applies only to anxiety, emotional pain, and the like. However, it is a startling thought that healing intelligence is also repressed from entering consciousness by the ego. It is as if there is an active filter and repressive mechanism at work which opposes and undoes it. Why? Because healing intelligence will disrupt the prevailing status quo of the ego, including its need and custom to organize itself around anxiety.

2. There are parts of the psyche that resist being healed. Complexes can present major difficulties in even being brought to consciousness, never mind their resistance to change. Even after transformative work has been done they can still reassert themselves. They seem to have wills of their own. The view that the psyche consists of different parts, some promoting and others resisting healing, is useful at this point.

3. The subject may not be ready for healing in all its aspects. There may be an ability to listen and align to the deep psyche but the capacity to integrate its material and engage in character

reform may be limited. To facilitate greater understanding of this point the total psychotherapy process has here been broken down into four stages with the last stage of integration divided into three parts. Previous pages argue and illustrate by case studies how problems at any juncture may impede growth and transformation.

4. The depth of some wounds makes healing difficult, sometimes impossible—they may only be modified or tolerated. When wounds cannot be healed at a deep level then other areas of the psyche need to be strengthened so the impact of the wound is lessened. This clearly takes time and can generate resistance. For example, a deep wound to the sense of self may, in some cases, be compensated for only by the development of a spiritual dimension to the psyche which may generate its own set of resistances.

5. It is difficult to face one's real suffering. A depression tends to shield the subject from real pain but thereby worsen the sense of malaise. Frequently, there are other emotions underlying the depression, such as anger or despair, that are difficult to bear. Their persistence impedes healing intelligence.

6. Many people do not know the way out of their emotional pain, or lack help. They may live in a culture where access to the inner world is not encouraged. They may have a value system which is excessively orientated to achievement and worldly success. Spiritual values may be absent, distorted, or even persecuted. The cultural milieu is very influential. The dominance of economic systems with great emphasis on wealth, science, technical training, and rational medicines can militate against the very notion of healing intelligence that escapes ego consciousness and its assumed control.

7. Healing might entail changing social relationships and this can be difficult. As healing is generated, changes in character, attitudes, and values ensue. This may require different relationships with friends and family and in more radical circumstances it may require moving on entirely.

8. Healing challenges addictions and, clearly, resistance can be powerful.

9. Healing requires energy and in the case of depression this is precisely what is lacking.

10. The loss of loved ones may cause wounds that are difficult to heal because the subject holds on to the suffering as the only remaining connection to the lost person. To be healed feels as if to lose the loved one. Resistance, therefore, appears like a form of love.

11. Deep wounds may require a transpersonal healing energy which is not commonly available.

12. Defences, as elaborated by psychoanalysis, are mechanisms to defend from anxiety or pain. Anna Freud (1937) explained a large number of these on a spectrum from pathological to mature. Defences can be embedded deep in the personality and are largely, often totally, unconscious. They are an obstacle to healing intelligence and the alignment to the deep psyche.

In short, resistance to healing and growth can be pervasive and deep-rooted. This is more than just the result of repression but includes a variety of factors, internal and external, collective and individual, even social and economic. Working with this phenomenon of resistance is core work for practitioner and client. These obstacles illustrate the obvious difficulty of undertaking the healing journey alone.

In summary, healing intelligence is a multifaceted presence throughout the psyche as it is in the body. While there may be one ultimate source underpinning it, its manifestation and operation reside in multiple centres. Healing intelligence takes place both unconsciously and consciously and can be activated in a number of ways. There are many obstacles and resistances to healing intelligence which are inevitably encountered in any serious transformation process. Ego consciousness plays a variable part throughout this drama and while its suspension is necessary at certain times, its active participation is part of the full healing process. There is a Jungian tradition that healing comes from the Self. However, viewing the psyche in three parts (consciousness, personal unconscious, and collective unconscious), it appears that healing intelligence is contained in all parts. It is undoubtedly true that the Self, in the collective unconscious, is the most powerful healing source. But also the personal unconscious, containing personal complexes, has its own healing centres—many case studies have been given of where the centre of suffering in the body, containing the complex, if approached correctly, can undergo a healing and transformation process. In addition, consciousness itself has healing components within it.

While the ego and its defences can block and filter the deeper psyche and healing impulses, inner awareness, like meditational awareness, is a portion of consciousness turned inwards in a pure non-judging manner. This part of consciousness, only activated when the rest of the mind is still, switched off, exhausted, or incapacitated, can look inwards at its own complexes and sufferings so they can express themselves and heal; it also can invoke and allow healing intelligence from the deepest areas of the psyche, the collective unconscious, to help this process. All three major parts of the psyche, therefore, are involved in healing intelligence and it is in their unified operation, in the *wholeness* of their functioning, that the full power of healing lies.

CHAPTER SIX

Integration with the spirit

There are some who by nature have strong spiritual components to their personality, just as others have a strong practical, theoretical, or interpersonal orientation. If these spiritual components are neglected such people may remain unfulfilled, even spiritually crippled. This is an immense topic and this chapter gives a few examples of the natural urge for such integration that comes from within the psyche.

Case study. John and his compass

John had substantial emotional damage but had found a creative link to sustain him. He was acquainted with chakra work and found it congenial to his spiritual, emotional, and psychological growth. He was, on his own admission, inherently fragile and in therapy we had passed some time understanding the circumstances creating this as well as the sufferings that ensued. We came to understand that an important way of strengthening himself was to be more in touch with his spiritual self. Not recognising this, then, he would be continually at odds within himself and vulnerable to stress. If, however, he was in touch with it he was stronger and more confident. This knowledge was revealed to him in a series of dreams. Here is just one:

> I am lost in a city, surrounded by noise, traffic, and danger; I know the beautiful countryside lies to the south but can't figure out which way this is since I am in the middle of tall buildings with no direct sunlight. I put my hand into my inner pocket and find a compass with which to orientate myself.

Comments: John needed continual reminding, from his dream world, his vision material, and his therapy, that he had an inner compass which could guide him—his daily spiritual practice. This example shows a case where someone needs to be reminded by the Self of the deeper or higher part of his nature, his guidance system. Integration of this part of his nature with consciousness is required. It will also be obvious to anyone who has struggled with spiritual matters that spiritual or healing experiences need to be remembered, brought back into consciousness so as to realize their potential within the personality.

An integration or linking is required between two parts of the psyche in order for a new centre of the personality to develop. In the simple example above, a reminder from the Self that the subject's ego needs to be nearer his spiritual centre, that the position of the ego on the ego-Self axis needs to shift nearer to the Self, is indicated. Jung's term for this intermediary position is the transcendent function. These reminder dreams are very common for spiritually minded people, especially those who have had uplifting and transformative spiritual experiences. A part of the psyche, referred to as the higher self by Sufis, makes a call, a reminder to the ego not to forget it. It reminds the dreamers or visionaries of their higher nature, or real nature as some would say. It is not clinically prudent to automatically interpret these inner experiences as defences, escapes, and unreal longings. On the contrary this contact with the higher self should be encouraged and developed within the context of an evolving self-examination and integration process. Just as the existence of creativity in a client is a good prognosis for therapy, the ability to contact the higher self can be the most useful of allies. Genuine spiritual components of the psyche can help clients when they are depressed, lost, and confused, playing a vital role in the work of realisation and integration. When such clients are in a state of suffering, the practitioner may help by reminding them of their access to the higher self which can be a continual support throughout their lives.

However, a word of caution is appropriate. In some cases a spiritual dependency may signify a vulnerable ego structure. When the ego and character components associated with it are damaged and in a chronic state of suffering then the subject may turn to the spiritual realm in order to fill the vacuum of the weakened ego and to repair the damaged emotional structure. Instead of progressing in a profession or having a network of friends or developing a central intimate relationship, such people may substitute normal ego support with spiritual support. These are difficult cases and generalisations are not prudent but a potentially useful strategy is to attempt to lessen the overdeveloped spiritual function and strengthen the underdeveloped ego functions.

Previous chapters have shown how certain techniques can be used in aligning to the deeper psyche. Those mentioned included meditation techniques, light trance states, active imagination, emotional expressiveness (for Jung, immersion in the emotional complex), shadow work, dream work, and imaginal body work. Many others exist. Below we mention chakra work in a little more detail since it coincides with the type of work described in these pages.

There are therapists who work with the type of imaginal body work described here simply because it is a very effective way of tapping into deeper emotions, as well as intuitive and sometimes visionary states. Dream work can be complementary to this type of work. With respect to imaginal body work it appears that the location of pain in various areas of the body frequently corresponds to what the Hindus, for millennia, have referred to as chakras. The methodology and belief system behind chakra work is more profound than that of light trance states and of locating emotional pain in the body, since it has an ancient Eastern, spiritual, and philosophical system attached to it. Chakra knowledge, spreading from the East into Europe since the 1920s, has become extremely popular in spiritual groups in the Western world and it is now used extensively in spiritual practices by those sympathetic to Eastern spirituality. The Hindu names of each chakra and a brief indication of their attributes are given below.

Muladhara: located between the genitals and the anus, it is associated with basic human potentiality and instincts such as survival.

Swadhistana: seated in the stomach and associated with sexuality and reproduction, it is inherently relational. It is I and you. The sense of identity is bound up with approval from the other. Questions of relationship dominate the psyche at this level. In its positive aspect it manifests as a sense of security, in its negative aspect as deep fear and anxiety.

Manipura: located around the solar plexus; positively, it is associated with one's sense of identity, power and will—the heroic ego; when damaged, fractured, or wounded it manifests negatively as a lack of internal coherence, strength, and confidence.

Anahata: the heart chakra, container of feelings, love, complex emotion, compassion, sense of self-balance and well-being. This chakra has great healing power, which is to say it can heal wounds in other chakras. However, it is also very vulnerable since many of love's wounds are lodged here and they may overpower its healing energy.

Vishuddha: located in the throat and a centre of expressiveness, creativity and communication. Blocked feelings and suppressed tears can manifest in this area.

Ajna: the brow chakra, centre of intuition, illumination, and awareness. This has the capacity to scan all lower chakras; it possesses tremendous healing power and can manifest its awareness as light. Its location is between the brows. Sensorially, it can at first be experienced as an itching or pressure; visually it can be experienced as a light, or a light within a cloud, but very rapidly it transcends space/time constrictions; it can begin as a locus or point, become an expansion, then a universality.

Sahasrara: the crown chakra, synonymous with the purest consciousness and supreme spirituality.

A quick glance at the attributes of these chakras will make clear their suitability for psychological work. First, the first five are connected to a range of emotions commonly experienced in psychotherapy. Second, some of them manifest blocks or complexes in a revealing manner in that they are relatively easy and rapid to access via inner visualization work. Third, they are located in the imaginal body and, as noted, this is a big advantage because it helps move one out of everyday ego-consciousness into the deeper psyche. Fourth, chakras possess self-healing energy which is augmented when they are approached by inner awareness, as in meditation. In addition, some chakras have healing impact on other chakras; the heart and especially the brow chakra are capable of this. The heart, naturally, uses love and life forces to achieve this healing while the Ajna or brow chakra possesses intuitive power and a healing energy of transcendental quality. The mobilisation of inner awareness is central to these healing processes when they have become blocked. Thus, a working knowledge of chakras indicates not only a more precise location of wounds, complexes, and emotional suffering than is commonly available in psychotherapy but also indicates the location and mobilisation of powerful healing energies in specific parts of the psyche. This "psychic technology" is ancient knowledge in Hindu culture.

All of the first five chakras partake of the realm of emotional disturbance and healing. The sixth chakra (brow or Ajna) is not consciously a part of most normal psychotherapy practice. However, in so far as deep intuition or illumination may occur in the course of the work, these may be attributed to this area. In my experience, a careful approach to this chakra can be most illuminating during the "scanning" process. Chakra work can be integrated into the type of psychotherapy work outlined here and, moreover, is something usually welcomed by clients of a spiritual disposition.

As an example of how there can be opposing areas of the deep psyche, indeed of different chakras, consider the following.

Case study. Jack and the smoke screen

Jack spent a year in therapy and was recovering from the death of his wife. During this time he had learnt to manage his intense grief and find new inner resources. Among these was chakra work, which brought him considerable measure of healing. During one of his down periods, when he was completely out of touch with his inner world, adopting a self-pitying attitude to himself, I reminded him of his access to other parts of his psyche which had proved of considerable help over the past year. He requested we do a scan. Instead of now slumping in the sofa, he sat upright, began focusing on his breathing and within moments, after a few words from me, let go of his worrying and self-pitying attitude and entered into his deeper psyche with his inner awareness intact and vital. I asked him to let me know if he felt this sense of self-pity and depression in any parts of his body and immediately he identified his throat. I asked him to focus on this area with his inner awareness, not interpreting or analysing, simply being aware. He reported he could feel the weight of this self-pity and depression but after five minutes it was clear it was not shifting but was firmly fixed. Significantly, his inner awareness of this chakra was not sufficient to produce a healing response and a change in tactic was required. I reminded him of his sixth chakra which he had previously contacted. He had little difficulty mobilising it once more and it seemed to expand from a single point of light to a general luminosity. I then asked him to bring this energy down to the throat to meet his self-pity. He struggled for a while and said all he could encounter was mist; he wanted to give up. Normally, I accede to any request to retire from a scan but in this case I strongly suspected this was just plain resistance, that depression should not win this struggle so easily. So I encouraged him to return to the sixth chakra and descend once more to the throat area. Again, he reported a mist and then said he could see nothing. I suggested he simply stay where he was in this experience and bring his full inner awareness to bear on proceedings, as well as on the presence of the sixth chakra. He spoke of a struggle, as if between different beings, within the mist. Five minutes later he said things had changed and he was feeling much better. We exited the scan. I saw him three weeks later and he said he had been in good spirits ever since our session. Here we observe what takes place, for the most part, unconsciously in the psyche: two opposing areas in struggle for dominance—one positive, another negative. In this case the negative (depression) would have won if the positive side had not been mobilised. The reason why John felt better was because his sixth chakra was activated and supported by the therapist, thus overcoming the dominance of his depressive tendency.

Comments: some readers might find reports of inner experiences such as these rather fantastical. I agree. In *The Transcendent Function*, Jung, after describing some of his techniques, pauses as he considers the probable reactions to his techniques. "The methods for bringing the unconscious to consciousness may strike the reader as novel, unusual and even rather weird" (p. 157). The inner world, experienced in such visionary states, consists of images, symbols, stories, and metaphors which are identical to the dream world. They are indeed the world of phantasy: dramatic, over-determined, humorous, apparently absurd or nonsensical but on closer inspection full of meaning. One can inter- pret them in exactly the same way as dream images. However, the vital difference is that visionary, inner states allow the activation of inner awareness which is a direct participation of a part of consciousness in the drama. It may also be surprising that one "unhealthy" part of the psyche puts up a strong resistance to another healthy part, yet this is no stranger than the resistance one can feel to doing physical exercise. What the above drama reveals by way of precise location—the throat (a clogged, self-concerned, emotional area in this case) versus the brow (a clear, illuminative one)—is a struggle in the psyche. Depression and self-pity can be subtle and powerful in resistance, easily throwing up a smoke screen, a mist, blocking illumination and clarity.

It is my understanding that any of the three great contributions of the East—meditation, yoga, and chakra work—to recent spiritual practices of the West can be incorporated with the emotional and spiritual work of psychotherapy. They are all centrally concerned with human suffer- ing and healing, they suspend normal ego functioning, activate inner awareness, align the subject to the deep psyche, and promote transfor- mational movement in the psyche. The application of certain spiritual ideas and practices to the work of psychotherapy is, then, feasible under certain conditions. There are also those of a determined spiritual nature who require nothing less than a psychotherapy which actively embraces core spiritual values. Psychotherapy with a spiritual dimension may fruitfully incorporate certain ingredients of Eastern traditions.

As well as the greater integration of the ego with the deep psyche there can also be a linking of different parts of the unconscious, as we have observed in the above case study. In chakra terms it involves a coming together of chakra centres. There are exercises done by spir- itual practitioners linking the chakras one to another. Tantra work deals with a movement of the life force from the spine to the crown of the head; Tao involves a *circulation of the light* and implies a movement of the vital energy (chi) around the "body". These are provocative metaphors for the psychotherapist working with a spiritual dimension. In these cases the unity is, to repeat, not just between the ego and the deep psyche, but rather of various parts of the deep psyche. Moreover, as the Tao philosophy illustrates, there is a dynamism, a movement of an essential life force (light, consciousness) between these centres. As an example of this process consider the following case.

Case study. Movement between chakras

Graham told the following:

> On a visit to a country manor I pass through a small door and enter an adjoined but hidden room which is quiet, holy, and beautiful. This experience is very moving.

Graham passed only a little time talking of this in the session, which chiefly concerned his feeling of being disorientated and ungrounded. In a scan he found his heart chakra to be like the adjoining room. I enquired about the brow chakra; he let an awareness of it grow, so it seemed to open and expand into the heart chakra, bringing great light and radiance. This took about twenty-five minutes.

Comments: his basic presenting problem in session was a feeling of disorientation. This could have resulted from various outside pressures upon him, but from the psychological and spiritual point of view it was because he was disorientated within. In the scan, his heart chakra presented the image of the quiet room. Here was the area holding the clue to his problem and its solution. At this stage, it was not clear what the room meant. However, the evocation of the sixth chakra, centre of intuition, its descent and partial union with the heart chakra, brought light in the room, the coming of awareness into this quiet space which lay hidden within him, much as the room lay hidden, adjoined to the house. His feeling of radiance and peace was the result of this unity he felt within, this inner space now receiving light. His feeling of disorientation disappeared. It signified that his spiritual potential, symbolised by the room, not only needed to be brought into consciousness, but needed to be filled by the light of his higher self. By such means he could feel less disoriented and more united in himself.

Such integration is both a psychological and a spiritual experience. The quiet room therefore represented the stillness required of his psyche so that higher healing forces in the psyche could be activated.

At first glance the above case study appears a straightforward example of spiritual integration, a remembering of the spiritual dimension by the ego. However, what made the integration effective was the manner in which the sixth chakra entered the fourth. This allowed a deeper integration to take place than a simple remembering by the ego could have achieved. Integration is therefore likely to be longer lasting when there is a coming together of different parts of the deep psyche; it is integration within the deep psyche itself, promoted by inner awareness.

The Hymn of the Pearl

Reminder dreams or visions are ubiquitous in the world's literature; the Hymn of the Pearl is one example. This beautiful story has had many titles, including Hymn of the Soul or Hymn of the Robe of Glory (an abridged version of the narrative by Jonas (1958) is given in the appendix). It comprises a section of the apocryphal Acts of Thomas, written originally in Syriac around the first century BC. There are many derivatives of this hymn, a parable in the New Testament being one of the most famous:

> The kingdom of heaven is like treasure hidden in a field, which a man found and covered up; then in his joy he goes and sells all that he has and buys that field.
>
> (Matthew 13:44)

In recent times there have been variations on this tale—in the nineteenth century Wagner's cycle of four epic operas, *The Ring of the Nibelung*, or in the twentieth century Tolkien's fiction, *The Lord of the Rings*. The Hymn of the Pearl readily fits into Christian or Gnostic interpretations.

The tale centres on the son of the King of Kings who is sent by his heavenly parents to "go down into Egypt and bring the One Pearl which lies in the middle of the sea which is encircled by the snorting serpent." He takes off his heavenly robe and departs on the difficult and dangerous road to Egypt where he plans to take the pearl from the serpent as it sleeps. To this end he stays nearby at an inn where he is surrounded by strangers, whom he fears may recognise him as not of themselves; they may suspect he has come to take the pearl and rouse the serpent against him. Indeed, they do recognise him as not of their own, but their strategy is to dupe him with wine and meat until he forgets his origins, and even the pearl … "Through the heaviness of their nourishment I sank into deep slumber." In grief, his parents and other great ones in the heavenly kingdom write him an impassioned letter reminding him of his heavenly origins and urge him to complete his mission and return with the pearl. Upon this reminder, he awakens from slumber, remembers his origins and mission and proceeds to engage the snake, lulling it to sleep by chanting the names of his heavenly parents, until he seizes the pearl and returns to his true land and his heavenly family. There he is greeted with great honour and again puts on his heavenly robe.

From a Christian perspective the soul has been captured by Satan (the serpent) and is prevented from going to its heavenly home. It is immersed in the fleshpots of Egypt, in drunkenness and sensuality. The remembering is the call of the divine to the soul to return to the divine whence it came. For the Gnostics a similar theme is embodied in this tale. For them, the soul, as a particle of light, is inevitably lost and immersed in materiality (the serpent), in the world of darkness; a great remembering has to take place. Humans have been duped, drugged, and have fallen asleep, existing only in stupor and ignorance. They must heed the call. Yet the human being cannot simply decide to return to his higher home, as this is not a decision of the ego. He has to retrieve something vital which is in the possession of the serpent, otherwise he cannot be complete.

Like all powerful symbols the pearl is full of meaning. Its richness is that it defies categorisation. The archetype of the Self may be thought of as the pearl of great price. It is held by a serpent, that is to say, in the unconscious, in the depths of the psyche. The searcher for this wholeness easily gets lost, forgets his purpose or becomes immersed in the world and its ways. He forgets his journey towards wholeness and enters a state of suffering. In order to find this pearl it is necessary to encounter the serpent (or the dragon in some tales) and a meeting with the shadow is required. Like many such meetings there is failure on the way and the shadow proves subtle and powerful. Thus, a remembering of one's higher self is required since the ego cannot accomplish this by itself. The higher self reminds the ego, bound as it is in the shadow and materiality, that it has a higher purpose and origin. It is not meant to be unconscious but to be fully aware of the whole range of its powers which includes the higher self.

From this perspective, the task is not to conquer the serpent or dragon, so frequently emphasized in Western stories, but *aprochement* and learning. In order to extract the pearl, it is necessary to listen to the shadow, to extract its light. One has to really listen to the shadow and learn. The serpent is not therefore an evil creature, but a symbol of many things including the unconscious, healing energies, instincts, life force, and transformation. A poignant part of the tale tells of the hero recounting the names of his family in the heavens and the serpent being lulled to sleep, thereby releasing the pearl. This can be interpreted, for the purposes of this book, in at least two ways. First, the impact of pure awareness on the shadow can be tremendous, releasing not only information but also the healing energy lying within it. Second, the mobilisation of higher powers, say from the sixth chakra, can have dramatic results with shadow material; or the heart chakra approaching another, which is in pain, may have remarkable healing effects. In these cases higher powers, healthy energies, or centres in the psyche may have a beneficial impact on areas of pain and darkness. The released pearl is wholeness, the integrative capacity of the psyche, which includes its healing (wholeness-making) functions. One of the layers of this story is the integration of light and darkness and this is of significance at four levels: metaphysics, mythology, spiritual experience, and psychotherapy. These will now be touched on briefly in turn.

First, metaphysics. A significant part of the metaphor of metaphysical speculation is in terms of light and darkness. Since the Hymn of the Pearl was formulated in Gnostic and Christian traditions one can expect a dualistic emphasis in which these two realms are kept largely apart, hostile and threatening to each other. It's as if to embrace one means to deny the other; in other words it is a split. However, if one looks on this tale more esoterically and with an Eastern eye, the darkness and light may be experienced as being an interconnected spectrum in which vital energies flow from one end to the other. The serpent now has the pearl, not because of its being stolen, but because life's energies are contained within it (the serpent) and develop from it. Conversely there must be some darkness or absence in the heavenly light for how could the heavens not have this most precious pearl? From this point of view, both sides of this apparent polarity need one another, are communicating and interconnected.

Second, mythology. This particular myth can also be developed or interpreted esoterically. The hero may approach the serpent and learn from it; Egypt is not simply a lower realm; there is powerful magic in this land. Also, when he creates the spell of the names of his heavenly father and mother, this is not simply an exercise of power over the serpent but an integration experience in which the higher and lower are joined. This is the essence of this viewpoint: the pearl, contained by the serpent, in symbolising wholeness, represents the potential integration of the higher and lower, the light and dark.

Third, spiritual experience. Light and darkness are perennial experiences of spiritual practice; I hesitate to say they are metaphors. Spiritual experience, when lying outside ordinary consciousness, cannot be encapsulated by the words invented by consciousness; they inevitably fall far short of the experience. It is better to say that these experiences of light and darkness are symbols in the sense used by Jung, images only partially knowable. Certainly, they can be experienced in the inner world with such intensity and reality that they can be transformative. The sixth chakra, for instance, can be experienced as a light which has healing properties and scanning ability. It cannot be confined to one point; it can pierce the darkness and bring about healing. Work on the shadow is vital so that the positive transformative feelings at its centre can be released from the surrounding negative, protective shell.

Fourth, psychotherapy, as presented here, can also be thought of as working with light and darkness. Many psychotherapists would have no trouble in saying they work with darkness and negativity in the psyche. It is more difficult to recognise that one needs to work with the light. Higher aspects of the psyche may be included here, such as intuition, illuminative power, love, forgiveness, compassion, humour, compacted meaning, wisdom, healing intentionality, an impulse to greater wholeness, a drive for growth and integration. Some of the healing qualities of the psyche, such as the heart and brow chakra, typifying the power of love and transcendent intuition so stressed by Assagioli, are remarkably transformative. In order to release the hold of darkness, negativity, and unconsciousness on the psyche, it is necessary to bring inner awareness to bear upon that area, especially if it is manifesting itself in pain. There are few useful results to be obtained by splitting off from it unless it is profoundly disturbing material. The purpose is to bring the pain to consciousness. In so far as psychotherapy brings only conscious understanding to bear upon the negativity in the psyche, however, it achieves a limited result—greater understanding but little, if any, healing. It is necessary to bring inner awareness to it. It is not a matter simply of analysing it, but rather of bringing a special, open, inner awareness, a light within the psyche, to bear upon this darkness. Those who work in psychotherapy with a spiritual dimension, both client and therapist, therefore can be said to work with darkness and light. Let us examine this further.

The negativity and suffering of the psyche is the dark matter requiring transformation. But how? This occurs, not by external pressure, nor through religious dogma, nor by the models of psychoanalysis and psychotherapy (which are but one context for the drama of healing), but by bringing into focus an inner possibility that the psyche has the power to heal itself. It may do this by constellating inner awareness, an inner light, and bringing it to bear upon the area of suffering which is largely unconscious and in darkness. If approached in this way then this darkness can reveal its secrets, open up its energy, and begin the process of transformation. This can be experienced as a light which has come from the darkness. The resulting new orientation in the psyche can be totally surprising. No one can predict what happens when this darkness releases its information, feelings, and energy; it is unique for each individual and is a beautiful experience. With words such as "beautiful" one enters into higher aspects of the psyche; and this is precisely what happens. The emerging potentiality has beautiful, energetic, and wonderful aspects to it. Higher experience, light, is locked up and contained in the darkness or, put conversely, the darker aspects of the psyche have, under certain conditions, the emergent properties of light. The darkness and negativity within the human psyche are not always transformed by the proximity of this inner awareness alone. Sometimes, more is required. In these cases, other parts of the psyche, whose vital energy has not been damaged by negativity, may help. Examples have been observed of this in the case of the heart and brow chakra regions. This is experienced frequently as an inner light coming to the area in darkness, bringing healing and happiness, wholeness and health.

We can translate the key symbols of the Hymn of the Pearl into terms useful for our theme, bearing in mind they can also translate into many systems of thought and religion since the tale is archetypal, spanning human generations and cultures, referring to something of enduring significance in and for the psyche.

The son of the King of Kings may be thought of as human consciousness, the centre of the drama. The heavenly kingdom and its occupants are the higher powers of the human psyche such as transcendent intuition, illumination, revelation, love, and transformative feelings. Egypt characterises the unconscious, especially in its sensual and material aspects. The serpent, located in Egypt, represents the darker, shadow side of the psyche, linked to instinct and nature. However, this area holds the pearl, the symbol of wholeness, which is the potential, integrative, and healing power of the psyche. It is unexplained why the heavenly Kingdom does not hold the pearl but needs to gain it. Has it been lost or captured? Or is the higher realm simply deficient when not having the energies of the lower realm? It lacks its most crucial ingredient, wholeness. There is, thus, a drama from the start of this tale, a division, an opposition, a lack, something to be made whole and good, to be healed. It is the task of human consciousness to achieve this. The son forgets his origins, the higher powers, and becomes immersed in materiality, unconsciousness. His mission is to possess the pearl, the wholeness of the psyche. He has to be reminded of his origins and the existence of the higher realm. Central to the drama is his approach to the serpent and obtaining the pearl. The shadow and darker parts of the psyche are what is worked with in the healing process but they contain the potentiality for wholeness and the possibility of integration. It is the integration of the higher and lower parts of the human psyche that is required. Human consciousness, represented by the son, is not capable by itself of realising this mission, just as the ego is not capable by itself of releasing the powers lying in the shadow. Inner awareness, enlightened consciousness, is the awakened son, reminded of his higher connections and capable of approaching the shadow which now uses inner awareness as its vehicle of expression and joins with the higher powers of the psyche.

The result is a human being who is a union of opposites, the higher and the lower. He is not identified with either exclusively since the higher realm of the human psyche is incomplete unless linked to the transformative energies of the lower, to instincts, shadow, pleasure, the body, and organic, natural life. Neither is he identified with only the lower realm since this means he is immersed in unconsciousness and the shadow, which needs to be liberated from its confinements and darkness by contact with the light. Both aspects of a human being need to be joined together, integrated, made whole—healed.

CHAPTER SEVEN

Questions and reflections

The reader may remember that this book was motivated by a "$64,000 question": "What is healing in psychotherapy?" This chapter will expand this unanswered question into a series of others which flow from it, each one followed by some reflections. It has a format like a conference in which questions are posed and replies are given. It will help the reader find briefer and more available material on the numerous questions that have come to mind as well as providing space for reflection on wider matters. Undoubtedly, this satisfies my long-standing frustration at not having an answer so many years ago. However, to confess, given the symbolic nature, inherent complexity, and elusiveness of the topic, my initial question and subsequent search has really turned into a longer series of other questions, each of which could be broken down into further questions themselves. Let me add the obvious. The $64,000 answer will never be given; but like the pearl of great price it can, I suggest, be experienced. Our knowledge in this field is necessarily limited; one can only reach so far into the unconscious, like wading out from the shore of an ocean.

What is a wound?

This is an area of intense, localised (in one part of the psyche) emotional suffering with a restrictive, debilitating, or possibly crippling effect upon the psyche. In severe cases, social and intimate relationships as well as behavioural functioning may be impaired. It may be unconscious or only partially known. It can turn into a complex, becoming a predictable and intense emotional reaction to certain triggers. In some cases, such as severe borderline conditions, the wound may not be localised but more globalised throughout the psyche, thus presenting a more serious condition.

What is healing intelligence?

No doubt, neurobiological research will continue to throw light on all aspects of the human psyche, including that of healing intelligence, but such work will do little, I suspect, to elucidate the "thing in itself". Belonging to the symbolic realm, it is observed in its manifestation; it has to be experienced not simply understood. To my way of thinking, it is almost impossible to think of the life process without this intelligence. All life forms possess it in the form of self-renewal, self-repair, and healing mechanisms; it is not a luxury in evolution but a necessity; life would not survive without it. Exactly the same applies to our bodies: healing intelligence, operating in numerous ways, is everywhere in the biological system, integrated in the fabric of genes and cells throughout the body (Chopra, 1989, p. 45). In the case of healing at a biological level, at first glance this may appear understandable: a cut stimulates the liver, which produces proteins to clot blood—a life-saving programme. However, on closer inspection many healing functions of the body have mysterious, almost miraculous qualities; the brain can sometimes repair itself, or DNA may heal its damaged information system, for instance. At higher levels in the human psyche, however, healing is not predictable, depending as it does on the cooperation of consciousness, which cannot be guaranteed. Healing, in its emotional and spiritual functioning, expresses itself in love as well as illuminative intuition; these are two of the most powerful forces in the human psyche, yet they can be very difficult to access. Healing intelligence—inbuilt, reparative, compensatory, and purposive—is a manifestation of the wholeness of the psyche and its natural functioning. It is facilitated by a healthy, strong potency in individual areas as well as in the total integrative functioning of the psyche. It is aided by a positive attitude of consciousness towards the deeper psyche.

How does healing intelligence work?

Emotional wounds are usually within certain parts of the psyche rather than being globalised; I find it useful to locate these in the imaginal body, emotions as they manifest in body centres; the chakra image of numerous centres is useful at this point. Presuming the repressive apparatus of the ego has been lessened there are, at least, six ways in which healing intelligence manifests itself:

1. Wounded areas of the healthy psyche may self-heal.
2. Wounded areas may be helped to heal by other areas of the psyche.
3. A healthy area may compensate for another area which is wounded, thereby providing some rebalancing and healing for the psyche as a whole.
4. Consciousness, especially in the form of inner awareness, ignites and stimulates the operation of healing intelligence when it makes sustained contact with the deeper psyche.

5. Healing intelligence, once engaged with and acknowledged, can reorientate consciousness by requiring attitude and character change.
6. Developed healing intelligence manifests itself in the integrative functioning of the whole psyche. The awareness and activation of this wholeness promotes healing.

Does the existence of healing intelligence ensure healing will happen?

Healing intelligence, conceived as originating in the Self, is a necessary but not sufficient requirement for healing to occur. Other necessary factors are character components such as optimism, emotional intelligence (Goleman, 2005), courage, determination, trust, and energy. The arduous work of integration is required to consolidate and actualise the gains offered by the emergence of healing intelligence, which requires the cooperation and availability of consciousness and positive parts of character structure in order to be effective.

What is healing in the psyche as an inner process?

Healing often takes place naturally and unconsciously in a healthy psyche. For those with a history of trauma and early disturbance healing energies can be depleted or non-operative, in which case strong protective mechanisms may come into existence. Most people naturally seek healing, in the first instance, from outside sources. When these are unavailable or insufficient the subject may possibly seek healing within. This journey has four broad stages: first, the honest expression of emotional pain; second, the mobilisation of awareness and its focus upon the area of suffering; third, the alignment to the deep psyche, allowing its healing intelligence to be operative; fourth, the integration of its wisdom and guidance into a reforming, growing personality. The task of healing and spiritual growth is to facilitate this inner dynamic rather than simply address the problems of the outer world, important though they are.

Is healing available to everybody?

It is available to many though, I believe, not all. It requires a number of conditions that may be difficult for some to meet. There are some who cannot engage in introspection, have no empathy, are totally removed from emotions, or have serious psychopathic, psychotic, or borderline conditions, making this journey unsought or impossible. It is naïve to presume that everyone even wishes for healing and growth. Some have difficulties with various stages of the process and for them complete healing may be unavailable. Although alignment to the deep psyche is possible, integration capabilities may be blocked. Nevertheless, healing is available to most people, sometimes even to those who seem most removed from it. The world's religions, which have always stressed the healing experience, are testament to this. It is also available to many who have no idea of how such a process works inside themselves or how they benefit. Generally it lies unconscious and freely available in the psyche.

Is healing a totally natural process?

Yes, it is a natural intelligence, not scientific knowledge constructed by consciousness and applied to the psyche. This does not mean it is automatic. Like healing forces in the body, it can be blocked, damaged, or overwhelmed. When blocked extra-ordinary measures may need to be taken for it to be activated. Consciousness may learn from the deep psyche what it is proposing in order to effect this healing.

Does healing have to be wrapped in arcane images or rituals?

Healing can lend itself to ritual and sometimes the arcane—witness many religious ceremonies. One cannot take away its mystery. The methods outlined here, and the comments made on the healing process, may, at times, seem surprising, but such is the nature of the unconscious. Healing intelligence lies naturally in the psyche, it is not a magical process caused from without, either by therapist or other agency, though, of course, it may be stimulated by them. Conceptually, the central ingredients of healing processes are easily grasped: suffering, inner awareness, darkness and light in the psyche are all accessible ideas. The difficulty is, of course, being able to work fruitfully with them.

Is it the same as Jung's concept of the individuation process?

The individuation process, starting with an examination of the personal unconscious and the persona, proceeding through the shadow, the anima or animus, archetypal alignment, and linking to the Self, is brought to consciousness effecting a generalised character reform in the second half of life. It is a general process of healing fundamental wounds. Blocks and distortions are addressed and a reorientation of consciousness toward the Self occurs. Rather than this overall, macro, broad-brush approach, the emphasis in these pages has been on healing as a more particular occurrence; numerous healing events in life are the stepping stones of the individuation path. Healing is a somewhat secondary concept in Jungian psychology, because the concept of individuation occupies centre stage. Once the individuation process is conceived of as having significant healing milestones then the concept of healing can be brought to the fore.

What is its connection to human suffering?

Suffering is the entrance to the inner world. Without this there would be very little inner exploration. Almost everyone approaches psychotherapy in order to deal with emotional suffering; few come with the explicit purpose of engaging in the development of their personality as conceived by the individuation process. Individuation starts with, and is fuelled by, the attempt to overcome such suffering. It is the attempt to heal oneself that characterises an intense, authentic, inner journey, otherwise the danger is that it remains an ungrounded, intellectual process. Transformational energy is the healing of suffering. In addition, knowledge of this inner process of healing can be applied to alleviate the emotional and spiritual suffering of others.

What is meant by the word soul? Is it the same meaning as the word spiritual?

Soul may be thought of as the deepest area of the human psyche, where attachment longings meet the numinous. Attachment refers to our feelings of love and all matters of the heart. It includes sexuality, in so far as it is linked with love, as well as the longing for transcendence. It connects one to a field far greater than the conscious self and ego. The word spiritual in these pages, therefore, means soul activity. It includes deep intuition, transformative feelings, revelation, illuminative experience, and love. It requires suspending the dominant functions and elaborate defences of the ego.

Does healing require a conscious engagement with the soul?

Healing intelligence in a healthy psyche is operative all the time unless it is blocked. For the most part it is unconscious. In many other cases healing takes place as a result of healthy and particularly loving interaction with others, more easily observed in a psyche which already has a degree of love within it. Thus, in the majority of cases there is no conscious engagement with the soul. But there are many instances of emotional wounds which do not heal by the above means. In these cases an active engagement with the soul can be required. This means that the deepest attachment needs are brought to the surface and explored; wounds are brought into consciousness; sexuality is examined as well as all desires and longings for partnership. In so far as this involves the healing of love wounds and the contacting of the higher forces of the psyche, such as transcendental intuition, then the soul is involved. Genuine spiritual longings greatly benefit from a conscious engagement with the soul.

What is its connection to human darkness, the shadow area of the psyche?

Dealing with human darkness is, naturally, the single most important ethical problem. It is foolish for any system of ideas, philosophy, or religion to think it has the upper hand over the dark areas of the human psyche. While the Jungian method of working with the shadow can be profound, in my view this is only for a minority of people who undergo an extensive journey of self-reflection. The most common way for the human shadow to be dealt with is by systems of religion and law which have rules and social structures. Bearing this in mind, the Jungian method, and the one I adhere to, looks not to condemn the shadow but strives to bring it into consciousness, to integrate it. It focuses on psychological development rather than control. Some of the case studies described here have shown that if the shadow is approached with a clear, inner awareness then it reveals both a meaning and a light which were previously hidden. It also contains within itself hidden, protected, and complex emotions. Light is, as it were, locked up in the shadow; or, to use more psychological terms, repressed but positive feelings may lie within the negative complex although a strong protective, negative defence may cover them. In the work of healing, just as in the individuation journey, working with the unacknowledged repressed areas of the psyche is vital for progress.

Can healing be achieved alone?

Psychological developmental stages take place in a social context. The healing process, for the vast majority, also takes place in such a context, especially through loving interaction with others. Those who require specialist help, guidance, and support, such as from psycho-therapists, are also in a social relationship, which is crucial for healing and integration. Thus healing, in this respect, is very difficult to accomplish alone. However, certain stages of the individuation journey can only take place on one's own. Becoming one's own unique self and establishing a dynamic ego-Self axis requires a joining up of *oneself* from within. It can't be done by imitating someone else. This is distinct from seeking wholeness as a unity with others outside of oneself. It is neither imitation nor modelling. One needs to be cautious however about exaggerating the extent of such inner work, especially for younger people since it is totally natural that human beings should seek to fulfil themselves in a love relationship; no amount of psychotherapy will compensate for this need. However, once the early development stages—relationship, and, possibly, reproduction—are completed, further progress requires individual development and, hopefully, one can become less needy of external support. There is therefore a natural balance and dynamic between social relatedness and individual development at different life stages. In particular, healing processes, as well as investigative exploration and meditation, in the early stages benefit greatly from being done with another person or in a group; synergies are clearly noticeable. In the later stages of life, providing the earlier stages are completed, a more individual approach to the inner world is required.

Are psychological defences a part of healing?

Psychological defences are a form of protection against emotional pain but are not part of the healing process. The psychoanalytic literature, which has pioneered our understanding of this, distinguishes two major types. Primary defences, such as psychotic denial, delusional projection, and severe splitting, defend the embryonic self before the emergence of an ego and are therefore embedded and radical. Secondary defences occur later, after the ego has formed, and defend it from destabilisation and threat from either within (the id in the Freudian schema) or without (the environment). Clearly, primary defences indicate early and more serious damage. They can prevent healing, for instance, by dividing the psyche into fractured and split off parts, and therefore the fundamental healing intelligence is inaccessible. Secondary defences, such as repression, projection, regression, denial, rationalization, and sublimation, prevent healing by their protection of the ego, thus impeding the healing forces of the deep psyche. Healing requires that defences are dropped and rigidity lessened so its intelligence can work.

Are there defences, resistances, or blocks to healing?

There are many sources of resistance or opposition to the healing process. These include an overdeveloped consciousness or rationality blocking the emotional and intuitive nature of the deeper psyche; parts of the deeper psyche actively resisting the healing impulse; a lack or failure at any stage of the transformation process, for example, an inability to link to the deep psyche or to integrate; a dominant depression or pessimism destroying any creative impulse to heal and transform; the difficulty of changing the external work or family circumstances in one's life underpinning and causing the problem; the power of addiction; an identification with the negative side of one's personality; the lack of access to proper knowledge, encouragement, help, or energy required to undergo the transformational process; cultural factors that are antagonistic to this way of thinking, as found either in materialistic society or in its opposite, a society heavily based on a rigid religious system. In short, resistance and impediments to healing and growth can be pervasive and deep-rooted.

By what energy are these blocks shifted?

Unblocking of healing and transformative energy mainly takes place as a result of two factors: first, the desire to diminish, finish with, or transform the intensity of personal suffering provides the essential motivation for change; second, the mobilisation of healing energy—released sources in the deeper psyche, previously neglected or repressed— provides the force for change. Within psychotherapy the commitment, energy, and belief of the practitioner are synergistic with the release of healing intelligence in the client.

How can we identify healthy material from the unconscious?

Not all dreams, visions, or contact with the unconscious reveal healthy material. However, healthy content can be recognised by its guidance function, extraordinary intuition, requirements for self responsibility, and personality change. It is also charged with meaning; the metaphors and symbols of important contents of the unconscious are multilayered. Frequently, dreams and unconscious contents are witty, structured as film or theatre scenes which have extraordinary locations, stories, and images. These contents of the deep psyche are largely concerned with the personal world of the subject. They not only represent problems of the past and present but look to the future, suggesting solutions which are usually to do with adaptations of the subject's character. Healthy contents from the deep psyche therefore are frequently purposive and intentional so the subject can move forward.

Are there transcendent sources of healing lying in the human psyche?

There are different sources of healing in the psyche, some being very "human" and generally to do with catharsis, sharing, and loving interaction with others. There are also, as Jung and Assagioli insisted, other sources of healing that are experienced as transcendent, awesome, and numinous, connecting one to forces outside of the normal conscious field. In Jungian terminology there is a connection to the archetype of the Self, which lies outside the ego. This connection promotes intuition, illumination, and transformative feeling functions, which can have an extra-ordinary dimension and occur in visionary and dream states central to the healing journey.

Are these sources sufficient for healing to take place?

As powerful as they are, these are frequently insufficient since there needs to be an integration of the material coming from these sources involving a reworking of the character of those who experience them.

Without this integration the numinous experiences can evaporate and fade. However, their role in the healing process is essential.

How is integration vital to the healing process?

The full healing process in psychotherapy, broadly conceived, is in three parts:

1. Contacting the deep emotions and complexes so as to allow their full expression.
2. Aligning oneself to the deep psyche and establishing a healthy ego-Self axis.
3. Integration of this material resulting from this meeting with the deeper psyche which involves character reform.

All three parts are necessary. Without integration the work of the previous stages remains limited and unfulfilled.

How does integration work?

Its essence is the fuller acceptance of all layers of feeling concerning wounds and complexes. It requires complete honesty and courage not only to realize these layers but to accept and then integrate them, which means to build them into one's consciousness so they are always accessible, not buried, denied, or split off. The core process is an inner journey, a self exploration, to examine what is really there and integrate it. There is a difference between doing this with one's conscious mind dominant and doing it with one's inner awareness switched on. The latter is the more effective path. Emotional and psychological health is required to work with this material and integrate it—a process of "re-membering". Spiritual components of the psyche may be activated to facilitate this process.

The above description refers to the integration of unconscious components with consciousness: one realizes and integrates the areas of suffering. There are deeper, more esoteric, aspects of integration by which different parts of the psyche become integrated with each other. For example, the heart chakra may integrate (join with) another area, such as the solar plexus chakra bearing pain. Or the brow chakra may integrate with a blocked throat chakra where a depression or despair may lie. These integrations can have excellent results upon complexes and areas of suffering. Again, the powerful vehicle for such change is inner awareness.

The extent to which first, consciousness unites (integrates) with parts of the deep psyche and second, different parts of the deep psyche link with each other, marks the progress of integration. Since the drive for such integration comes from outside of ego consciousness and can be seen in dreams and visualizations to derive from the deep psyche, then it follows that there is an archetype of order and growth, pushing for realisation, which can only happen when consciousness recognises, accepts, and integrates this entelechy.

Can Eastern methods such as meditation and chakra work be integrated with psychotherapy of a spiritual dimension?

Any spiritual work truly aligning consciousness to the deep psyche, be it meditation, chakra work, or yoga, can be incorporated with in-depth psychological exploration. Any method which activates inner aware-ness so that it contacts the deep psyche and allows its expression is a potential ally. However, the psychotherapy session should not turn solely into a meditation, chakra, or yoga exercise. Psychotherapy must take the lead. This applies not only to their positioning in the therapy session (i.e., meditation or chakra exercises should only be part of a session) but also in the way in which they are approached. For exam-ple, breathing and inner-awareness methods can be used to approach core complexes and emotional pain. They are used to temporarily by-pass the ego, suspend the conscious mind, create a still, listening space, and approach the troubled areas of the psyche with one's inner awareness. These meditation, chakra, or yoga methods, in the type of psychotherapy envisaged here, are not to avoid the areas of suffering but, on the contrary, to confront them and give them the maximum chance of healing. Integration is often the most difficult, neglected, yet underestimated aspect of the journey.

In those cases where someone wishes to engage in a fuller, more intensive exploration of such techniques as yoga or medita-tion, a spiritual group is more appropriate. Psychotherapy sessions are not principally spiritual exercises and should deal with the nitty-gritty of human psychology and complexes: the examination of suffering is their focus.

One way of incorporating a meditative-type practice, called the scan, into sessions has been described. Scans are preceded by considerable psychotherapeutic investigation of complexes, bringing them into consciousness, understanding their origins and functioning, and are followed by the work of integration. The method is therefore thoroughly in line with psychotherapeutic procedure. Its purpose is to facilitate the second stage of the healing journey, the alignment to the deep psyche. There may be many methods of achieving this but all are variations on a theme: the centring of consciousness around the contents of the deep psyche. Practitioners who use other or similar techniques such as dance, clay work, drama, drawing, active imagination, experiential focusing, other meditation techniques, yoga, and so on may formulate their own methods of integrating it with the psychotherapy they practice. Indeed, I accept there should be no one method espoused for accessing the unconscious. There is no single right way and individual practitioners should develop their techniques from their own healing experiences. According to this way of thinking, there will be many different methods employed by different practitioners reflecting the different paths of their own healing and development. As soon as psychotherapy training insists dogmatically on fixed practices then the path to the deep psyche is impeded. However, when many tens of thousands of practitioners are offering their services one can understand the pressures for uniformity, accountability, and transparency. But standard methods will not produce deep healing. Nevertheless, I believe there should be a shared context underlying whatever method is used to access the deep psyche. This includes the substantive work of analysis and integration that precedes and follows this access and alignment to the deep psyche.

Is active imagination a very different process from meditation in contacting the deep psyche?

Active imagination, a method personally favoured by Jung, involves a creative dialogue with the contents of the unconscious, especially with figures from the inner world. This occurs after the conscious, ego-dominated mind is suspended and the full emotional encounter with complexes and personal material eventually reveals the contents of the archetypal core. At this point, a new positioning of the centre of the psyche (the transcendent function), closer to the pole of the Self, now takes place. Meditation methods or experiential focusing techniques are gentler but still involve the suspending of normal consciousness and stress the method of inner awareness. This likewise facilitates the creative encounter with inner complexes and archetypal material. When used in the context of psychotherapy these are two different methods for achieving very similar ends.

Are chakras real?

All the key concepts used in depth psychology, such as the ego, the unconscious, and defences, are simplified models attempting to explain highly complex phenomena. The concept of chakra is similar but here one can think of it as a symbol. Although chakras are supposedly located in the spinal column—"subtle matter", rotating disks of energy pro-foundly influencing every aspect of the human being—none of them can be called real in the sense a leg or arm is real. It is better to ask if such concepts are useful: have they stood the test of time and do they lead to deeper enquiry? Many concepts coming from the East have been useful for thousands of years; chakras are described in the Upanishads, written over a thousand years before Christ, and had a long oral history before then. They are also peculiarly suited to a spiritual, psychological, and symbolic view, very compatible with modern spiritual thinking in the West. The question of chakra "reality" may be rephrased: does chakra symbolism help to contact the transformative powers in the psyche?

Does psychotherapy necessarily have a spiritual dimension?

Most of psychotherapy does not have an explicitly spiritual dimension; only certain sections do so. Even within those schools which embrace a spiritual dimension, not all institutes and groups practice it to the same extent. Most clients do not come to a therapist for spiritual mat-ters but do so for reasons of painful emotional suffering. Nevertheless, a spiritual dimension can provide the vital healing and transformative ingredient required for progress, although, in my view, this should not be promoted to the client as the only way forward.

Can Christianity be integrated with such healing processes?

In its more benevolent aspects with its emphasis on love, forgiveness, and higher transcendent powers, there are certain elements that can match psychotherapy with a spiritual dimension. Psychotherapy and counselling is now offered in parts of the Catholic Church. Also, the more arcane traditions of Gnosticism and alchemy have been shown by Jung to relate to the individuation process. The harsher aspects of Christianity, such as an insistence on sin and a highly judgemental ethical position, can be an obstacle to psychological exploration.

Can all religions be integrated with a spiritually orientated psychotherapy?

In so far as a religious or spiritual system creates a sacred space—be it through contemplation, prayer, meditation, architecture, ceremony, or ritual—its contribution can be integrated with this type of psychotherapy. The access to the deep psyche and its transformative energies has always been the province of religious and spiritual endeavour, whose practitioners are the historical, spiritual specialists. However, religious systems of mass acceptance may rapidly convert into ideologies and operate as instruments of control. Especially when evangelical or authoritarian, they become a hindrance to a genuine, open, authentic, inner journey. Even the moral codes of religious and spiritual movements, historically and socially indispensable though they may be, can be an impediment when imposed upon the living process of the encounter with the deep psyche. The injunction to love one's neighbour may be an obstacle if one actually needs to enter one's darkness and shadow to discover what is really there; the exhortation to surrender the ego may be counterproductive if what is required is that the ego and its platform of support should be reinforced not weakened; the recommendation to give up one's family and career may be damaging if it leads to psychological breakdown; the suggestion that one should concentrate on helping others is crippling if the subject does not know how to help himself. The moral perspective of the deep psyche is quite different from that of consciously constructed systems, no matter how ethically plausible they are. While the ego is, as a rule, selfish, the deep psyche is Self-orientated—clearly seen in dreams which so often contradict the orientation of consciousness and insist on a greater reality. This inner directing system and intelligence is concerned with the total psyche of which consciousness and its ego subject are only parts. Thus, from the perspective of the Self, the moral concern is that the ego is in harmony with the deep psyche not that it should be in harmony with the egos of others. This may account for the unusual moral perspectives and actions of those on a genuine path of spiritual growth; they do not follow normal rules and edicts because they are listening to and following the promptings of the deep psyche.

Psychotherapy may differ from traditional religions with respect to a number of issues. First, the shadow, from a psychotherapy perspective, needs to be explored and approached uncritically, not judged and rejected; second, sexuality needs to be brought fully to consciousness, revealing so much of the psyche (such as its deep attachment needs and longings), not treated judgementally; and third, the question of ethics, which, for the psychotherapy journey, needs to be developed from within and emerge later in the process, rather than being accepted from without and structuring the moral position from the start, as it is in many religions. Individual growth is a journey of discovery not the acceptance of externally imposed rules.

Are there particular psychological aptitudes or skills favouring the work of psychotherapy and healing?

Yes, such skills may be thought of as types of awareness required to progress from basic to advanced practice in psychotherapy and spiritual work. The more advanced of these are activated in healing-individuation experiences. Together they form a spectrum of intelligence of working in the inner world. These positive attitudes include: capacity for introspection; ability to contact and express deep emotion as well as accessing their truth; an ego with the capacity to link to the unconscious but also to be relatively independent; to see oneself more objectively; acceptance of self-responsibility; awareness that one's psyche consists of different inter-related parts; the existence of a metaphorical and symbolic attitude so as to contact and work with the deep psyche; the ability to mobilise inner awareness so that the deepest parts of the psyche, especially healing intelligence, can be reached.

For most psychotherapy, with perhaps more limited and achievable aims, not all of the above are required. All will be needed, however, for a complete psychotherapy which has a considerable measure of healing, character transformation, and individuation; the last two—symbol facility and inner awareness—are particularly activated in healing processes. When the client stagnates it is useful to consider which of the above may need developing.

What is the role of the psychotherapist in this healing process?

The practitioner provides a container for the healing process to unfold, contributing healing energy and experience. Psychotherapists deeply involved with healing are never anonymous figures since their personalities and healing energies are vital for the journey of the client. Clients may feel they know their therapists well at some deep level, although they know little about their personal life. The relationship between client and psychotherapist co-evolves with the integration of the psyche of the client. As this relationship deepens, the integration process within the client can move to new levels. Healing is stimulated by synergy, inter-reaction, and relationship. More specifically, it is a shared field that is constellated, within which the participants—therapist and client—enact their unique drama.

Is psychotherapy necessary for healing in the psyche to take place?

Care for the sick has taken place, as far as paleo-anthropologists can gather, throughout human history and beyond, back to early hominids. One of the earliest skeleton finds, dating from around 1.5 million years before present, is of a Homo Erectus female who died with an advanced state of a disease called hyper-vitaminosis A (Walker, 1982). It is not possible to survive this disease to such a stage without being cared for. This remarkable find suggests that care existed among Homo Erectus (our genus but a different species), which preceded Homo Sapiens by over a million years. Even at this early period, special treatment of the dead suggests concern for the grief of the surviving (Spikins et al., 2010). Another example is the skull of a ten-year-old child, (dating from 530,000 years before present) who was found to have had a debilitating birth defect called craniosynostosis (by which joints fuse in the skull before growth is finished, thus impairing brain development). Again, intense care must have been provided—an "ancient proof of the care of the socially handicapped" suggests Garcia (2010).

The archaeological record indicates that Neanderthals, half a million years ago, showed care of chronically ill individuals (Spikins et al., 2010). More recently, among Neanderthals and early Homo Sapiens, around 100,000 years ago, there are burials of the dead, so it is hypothesised that consciousness of individual mortality had evolved

(Leakey, 1992). Later, around 40,000 BC, precious objects and even flowers were buried with the deceased. In the history of human civilization, from the Egyptians onwards, there are advanced burial ceremonies, and beliefs in the after-life and resurrection. Healing myths lie at the heart of civilization and it is only reasonable to suppose that, given the precarious conditions of humanity throughout its history, concern for care, healing, and medicine has always existed. The New Testament shows the fascination for miracles of healing the sick, where little distinction is made between mental, physical, and spiritual malaise. The history of shamanistic practices clearly shows healing that embraced not only physical conditions but those of emotional or spiritual malaise.

Psychotherapy is a modern phenomenon. It arose in the late nineteenth and early twentieth centuries out of the spiritual vacuum created by the advance of enlightenment thinking. It is a highly individualized, verbal concentration on mental and emotional conditions, thus breaking from the more holistic tradition of earlier generations. Psychotherapy is a specific historical creation. Its individualised, dialogic form, and its methods of contacting the unconscious form a particular development for treatment arising in Western civilisation at a specific juncture. Healing has taken place for thousands of years without psychotherapy. Other forms of healing will come into being and replace this one, which, in the future, may seem as antiquated as alchemy. However, the process of individuation and healing is an archetypal journey and as such its broad features are shared with initiation, creation, healing myths, and rituals throughout human history. Psychotherapy has a unique contribution to make in this process because of its requirements for extensive character analysis and subsequent integration of the material arising from the unconscious.

Can psychotherapy also be a block to this healing process?

Rigid psychotherapy, over-intellectualised systems, poor training, all contribute to inadequacy of provision. Moreover, psychotherapy easily lends itself to mind dominance—an insistence to analyse, to use models, to understand, rationalise, and reduce phenomena—thereby reinforcing a spilt from the body, its energies and emotions. The very word "analysis" reveals its orientation. Psychotherapy may also be restricted by political correctness. Conceived of and practiced in a rigid and limited manner, psychotherapy can block access to the deeper psyche and its potential for transformation. The method outlined here of imaginal body work is only one step in the direction of contact with healing intelligence; many other radical and deep methods exist including those in other healing disciplines.

Is it necessary to adopt a model, such as the archetypes of the collective unconsciousness, to achieve healing?

Healing and growth in the psyche do not require the acceptance of any particular model of the psyche. However, it is common to adopt one in the early stages, for guidance on what can be a difficult and confusing path; ironically, the ego needs something to hold on to before it can let go. Belonging to a religious group can amount to the same thing. The model provides initial security and meaning but needs substantial modification and change as deeper work is engaged in. Jung outlined a theory of archetypes as underlying determinants of human character and consciousness. The classic pathway of a Jungian psychotherapy is said to progress through an encounter with these archetypes, the shadow, the animus/anima, and the Self in particular. Some therapists of a spiritual persuasion find such ideas illuminating. However, the core requirement, as presented in these pages, is simple inner awareness, a letting go of ego consciousness, a process of listening, attunement, and integration. Two of the most important ingredients of this process are, first, the quality, warmth, commitment, and enthusiasm of practitioners, no matter what their school; and second, the courage and dedication of the client. These qualities cannot be modelled.

Models and pre-conceived structures, although indispensable at the macro level to schools of psychotherapy, are not directly helpful to the healing and individuation journey at the micro level of psychotherapy. They are only indirectly helpful to the practitioner and can be a positive hindrance to the client. Every individual's pathway is unique. Models are conscious formulations of the rational mind. The deep psyche does not work according to formulae; it is dynamic and endlessly surprising. As soon as a model is imposed upon it this creative energy is hampered, goes underground, and can even become destructive when repressed and not allowed expression. The best approach for clients is to temporarily leave aside all models and preconceptions so as to enter an honest, unpremeditated meeting with their own suffering, complexes, and deep psyche. The best approach for the practitioner is to enter the consulting room leaving in the background such learnt models, so as to work with the living psyche. However, once out of the consulting room practitioners should, in my view, adopt a continual learning disposition and engage with the roots of their discipline. This is best done in a parallel process by working in depth with their own and their clients' psyches.

Can all wounds be healed?

Some wounds cannot be healed. However, there is an enormous difference between being unconscious of a wound and knowing it exists. Further development may require integrating and taking responsibility for it. It is a further leap to "work through" the wound. This may result in its reduction or even its disappearance. Different levels of healing are possible. Temporary healing is also of importance, for while the deep wound may return, its temporary diminishment allows growth to take place and prevents negative acting out, such as destructive attacks on close or intimate relationships.

What is the wounded healer?

This is one of the most persuasive descriptions of the healing practitioner. Ideally it refers to those who have transformed, but still consciously carry, their wounds, and are thus especially capable of helping others. This is its positive aspect. It can operate negatively when a wounded practitioner needs the wounded client to enhance a sense of identity. Creative sublimation of the therapist's wounds is frequent.

In what way can those on a spiritual path benefit from psychotherapy?

There are at least seven such benefits.

First, a thorough character analysis and the building of genuine self-knowledge is a foundation for spiritual work. Unless this is done the subject is likely to fall back into unconscious complexes and shadow material.

Second, in the spiritual journey subjects need grounding and rooting into their ordinary lives and character, especially when strong spiritual experiences are present. It is simply too tempting and dangerous to be carried away by transpersonal energy. Even for those well advanced on the spiritual path, it is easy to be overcome by complexes and become inflated (god complexes, megalomania, and the like).

Third, the contrary position is also true. There are many on the spiritual path who feel they cannot live up to their ideal, and a working through the roots of such problems in their character is required, rather than perpetuating a cycle of excessive projections on to spiritual leaders followed by disenchantment, guilt, or shame.

Fourth, an intensive psychotherapy insists on examining the shadow very closely, which is something that can be neglected on the spiritual path. Advantages of such work include greater self-knowledge, integration of the psyche, and release of energy that has been dammed up in the shadow.

Fifth, spiritual groups sometimes downplay the ego in favour of spiritual experience. Some Eastern methods recommend the transcending of the ego altogether. Psychotherapy is concerned that the ego is relativized and even surrenders its dominance. Fundamentally it looks for a readjustment and reshaping of the ego and its better alignment to the deep psyche.

Sixth, spiritual groups have more than their fair share of wounded people who are seeking healing through contact with the group itself. The knowledge of the roots of suffering in their character and early background is invaluable; they are seeking healing in the first place, owing to wounds in their psyche. In more serious cases of borderline and psychotic conditions an elementary knowledge of psychiatry and diagnosis is essential since not recognising the psychological roots of emotional disturbance and breakdown may be full of risk. Recommending that fragile people continue with ego-dismantling practices in the name of supposed spiritual advancement is ill-advised. When this is compounded by unrecognised psychological problems of spiritual leaders the consequences can be dangerous and sometimes fatal. Elementary psychological knowledge should be as available as a first aid kit.

Seventh, spiritual leaders may need particular help, not only to protect themselves from inflation and power dynamics, but also from the intensity of exaggerated projections put on them from their followers. They too suffer nervous breakdown, anxiety, paranoia, depression, and can benefit from help, especially when there is no one in their spiritual group to whom they can turn. Spiritual leaders may have problems of particular emotional and psychological concern. After all, why have they spent such time and energy in the healing process? The group should not provide the only pathway for their healing, which should be Self-generated.

Are there one or many sources of healing in the psyche?

The body has innumerable protection devices, defence systems, repair operations, and healing mechanisms. Some of these are simple to grasp while others are of immense complexity and beyond our understanding. It is difficult to comprehend or prove there is one central co-ordinator of this biological system of healing, though it may exist. Rather, it seems healing intelligence is distributed throughout the body and there are numerous ways in which it is activated and operates. Philosophically, such a view is pluralistic rather than monistic—there are many sources of multifaceted, healing intelligence rather than one.

Jungian psychology has both monistic and pluralistic possibilities: on the one hand, the Self is the archetypal centre of order, a unitary principle guiding the psyche—rather like the idea of one God; on the other hand, there are archetypes which have positive healing power.

From the healing perspective in this book there are widespread sources of healing intelligence in the psyche coming from different centres. Inner awareness, when brought into proximity of an emotional wound, can promote healing activity beginning with catharsis. Some wounds are capable of self-healing, while others may require the action of other parts of the psyche. To use the language of chakras, some centres—such as the heart or the brow chakras—possess healing properties influencing other centres that carry wounds. Healing intelligence may manifest itself through dreams and visions which are capable of reorientating the subject's life. It follows, therefore, that all levels of the psyche possess healing intelligence: first, consciousness has a portion of itself—inner awareness—that has healing properties when in contact with the areas of suffering; second, the personal unconscious, containing emotional centres that may have pain and trauma, is capable of self-healing or the healing of one centre by another; third, the collective unconscious, the deepest layer of the human psyche, possesses the most powerful source of healing intelligence, the Self.

In the practice of psychotherapy both these viewpoints (the monistic and the pluralistic) are useful and can be complementary: the Self as an inner, unifying director of numerous localised healing sources in the psyche. From the practitioner's point of view this is not a contradictory position.

Does psychological type influence the healing process?

The alignment to the deep psyche, the capacity to listen and absorb the messages of the inner world, the requirement of symbolic work, the necessity of intense emotional experience, clearly require an introverted orientation, and developed intuitive and feeling functions, typical of Jungian psychotherapy. Other therapies may stress different capacities, some requiring more emphasis on cognitive faculties or practical orientation, while others stress social relations and group work. From the Jungian point of view, thinking functions, though initially useful, can be a block to deeper alignment to the psyche, while the sensation function (practical and matter of fact orientation) needs to recede so that the less substantial but no less real, inner world can come to the fore. A dominant, extraverted function needs to lessen and an introverted orientation needs to develop. Myers-Briggs, following Jung, added the axis of perception versus judgement, the former indicating a tendency in some people to use looser flow states whereas judgement types require a tight structure to organize their mental world. Clearly the alignment to the deep psyche requires the former rather than the latter (greater perception rather than judgement), corresponding to Jung's stress on and preference for synthetic rather than analytic attitudes. In summary, the Jungian viewpoint is that access to the deep psyche is promoted by introverted and perception orientations as well as feeling and intuitive functions. However, while access to, and working with, the unconscious is promoted by these functions, the end result of healing and development often requires rebalancing of the psyche: thus the highly introverted may need to develop extraversion while the predominantly intuitive may need to develop more practical sensation functions; those who are mainly feeling-orientated may need to develop thinking processes, while those given to loose flow states may need to develop more structure and organization.

The healing process may be understood in a similar way. People tend to heal themselves using their dominant functions. Thus a feeling type may use the heart function first and foremost. One observes this clearly in scans and visualizations where access to heart energy is rapid and the power of its healing function is dominant. Similarly an intuitive type will find easier access to the sixth chakra, which is the centre of intuition, and this function may play a chief role in healing operations. Someone with an exaggerated thinking function has a distinct healing disadvantage. While lighter wounds may heal by themselves, deeper wounds will tend to be repressed. Such a person will need to develop the feeling or intuitive function in order to work more closely with the healing capacity of the inner world. If this proves impossible then the style of therapy should shift from emphasizing an inner world to focus on the relationship of the subject with family, friends, work, and so on as the vehicle to promote rebalancing change. Those with dominant feeling functions (using the heart chakra) may have a paradoxical disadvantage with regard to deep wounds. Their feeling functions and heart chakra may be so damaged by trauma or love's wounds that natural reparative capacities are compromised. Scans and inner work can portray it as a wasteland, a dead place, and here one is warned of a depletion of healing energy in the heart, which happens to be their chief healing function. In such a case, knowledge of the inner world and its dynamics can help, since by switching the emphasis to the sixth chakra and developing the intuitive function, this powerful centre can heal wounds in other parts of the deep psyche, including the heart.

How is healing connected with individuation and wholeness?

As opposed to more specific or localised healing, the individuation process posits a healing of the psyche as a whole. Here, many areas of the personality are involved. Some character components are challenged and recede while others are encouraged and come to the fore; the role of the ego is modified as the information, feelings, and energy of the deeper psyche are allowed to express themselves. Higher transcendent forces in the deep psyche may be freed and become operative promoting great change and reform. In particular, the acknowledgment of the existence of some other centre outside of the ego pressing for change, reform, and development is central. In other words, a number of components of the psyche which were previously underused, or neglected, become operative and integrated. Greater wholeness is achieved. The Old English word to heal—*hælan*—means to make whole, to restore to health (hal): thus the words *wholeness* and *health* reveal their common etymological root.

While wholeness necessarily implies a greater integration of different components of the psyche, the healing of the individuation process is an expression of the integration and intelligence in the psyche as a whole. The psyche is not simply an amalgamation of bolted-on separate components: its whole functioning is an integrated intelligence. The greater the alignment and integration of consciousness with this totality, the more advanced is the healing and individuation process.

What has love and death got to do with it?

Love is the supreme positive force of the human psyche and is the essence of the healing process: no love, no healing. Most psychotherapy concerns damaged relationships and love. Psychotherapy with a spiritual dimension focuses on how this love can be found in the inner world, independent of having to experience it in the outer—a form of love within the Self.

The natural course is to love another, of which the love between child and mother, and that of lover with lover, have always been considered supreme exemplars. This is a type of mirroring in which one's truth and essence is discovered, reflected back to oneself through the eyes of the beloved, and one's uniqueness experienced—one becomes alive. This eternal moment is captured in Winnicott's (1967, p. 112) inimitable description of the child who looks up into the eyes of his mother and sees himself in their loving reflection—himself in her. She, too, looks into his eyes and sees the reflection of herself—her in him. This loving interpenetration is a symbiosis, a mutual interpenetration, a sharing of essence, a dual unity. One's own individuality and separateness is temporarily annihilated in this ecstatic shattering of the ego. Beauty is its reality. Such love is an unconscious climactic for those fortunate enough to experience it; it happens without effort. However, so much of existence is lived in its shadow.

The wake-up call for love is death. For what is the essential that one can take into the night of death? Love is the only force one can take. Almost all who are about to die instinctually gather the love around them as a garment that can protect them. It is the only essential meaning at the end of life. No amount of fame or fortune can withstand this terrible reality. Only love and the knowledge that comes through love can do this. For those who do not have the good fortune of having loving others surround them in their death there are two other possibilities; first, the accumulated experience of love within oneself, the memories of those one has loved and been loved by; and second, to be in touch with the source of this love in oneself, to know the experience of loving oneself, the beauty of being alive and this life one has lived. The latter, though esoteric, is a possibility. It is, of course, better to realize this long before one dies—on the one hand to open the heart and practice love, and on the other to activate integrative, healing intelligence throughout the psyche, to experience healing and wholeness.

The Hymn of the Pearl

This is an abridged version from Hans Jonas' *The Gnostic Religion* (1958, pp. 113–116). The original poetic form (as it may have been sung as a hymn) has been put into a narrative.

When I was a child and dwelt in the kingdom of my Father's house and delighted in the splendor of those who raised me, my parents sent me forth from the East. They made a covenant with me, and wrote it in my heart that I might not forget it: "When you go down into Egypt and bring the One Pearl which lies in the middle of the sea which is encircled by the snorting serpent, you will put on again your robe of glory and ... be heir in our kingdom".

I left the East ... passed over the borders of Maishan ... came into the land of Babel and ... went down into Egypt ... I went straightway to the serpent and settled down close by his inn until he should slumber so that I might take the Pearl from him. Since I was one and kept to myself, I was a stranger to my fellow-dwellers in the inn ... Yet I clothed myself in their garments, lest they suspect me as one coming from without to take the Pearl and arouse the serpent against me. But through some cause they marked that I was not their countryman, and they mixed me drink with their cunning, and gave me to taste of their meat, and I forgot that I was a king's son and served their king. I forgot the Pearl for which my parents had sent me. Through the heaviness of their nourishment I sank into deep slumber.

All this that befell me, my parents marked, and were grieved ... they wrote a letter to me ...

"From your father the King of Kings, and from your mother, mistress of the East ... to you our son in Egypt, greeting. Awake and rise up out of your sleep, and perceive the words of our letter. Remember that you are a king's son: behold whom you have served in bondage. Be mindful of the Pearl, for whose sake you have departed into Egypt. Remember your robe of glory."

I remembered I was a son of kings. I remembered the Pearl and I began to enchant the snorting serpent ... charmed it to sleep by naming over it my Father's name, and that of my mother, the queen of the East. I seized the Pearl, and turned to repair home. Their filthy and impure garment I put off, and directed my way that I might come to the light of our homeland, the East.

My letter which had awakened me I found before me ... so it guided me with its light that shone before me, and with its voice it drew me on. And I cast the royal mantle about my entire self. I ascended to the gate of salutation and adoration. I bowed my head and adored the splendor of my Father who had sent it to me, whose commands I had fulfilled .... He received me joyfully, and I was with him in his kingdom.

GLOSSARY

Acting out Behavioural manifestation of unconscious conflicts and anxieties.

Active imagination A direct, creative relationship with figures from the unconscious rather than a passive or analytic observation of them. They may be talked to, even challenged; the inner world is regarded as totally real. A method used by Jung on himself as well as his patients.

Alignment The capacity of consciousness to link with the Self and archetypal components of the psyche.

Analytic A process of understanding, breaking into component parts, dissecting, understanding causes, origins, and how things develop. It usually characterises a reductive method of understanding the client's symptoms in terms of early family dynamics.

Archetypal realm The area of the deep psyche, outside of the control of the ego, containing archetypes and healing intelligence.

Archetype Inbuilt, psychic potential expressed in behaviour, thought, images, and creativity; universal in the human species.

Catharsis Feelings of relief and purging after the expression of suffering.

Client A term used by default in these pages to indicate the recipient of psychotherapy. It is not entirely satisfactory because it over-emphasises the commercial nature of the therapeutic relationship. The term patient, used frequently in psychoanalysis, is not used in this book since it is based on a medical model with an implied passivity of the client versus the authority of the doctor. Another term that has been avoided is *analysand* (sometimes used in Jungian circles) which over-emphasises the analytical aspects of psychotherapy.

Collective unconscious The deepest part of the psyche, universal in the human species; referring to the higher and lower elements, instincts and archetypes, libido and healing intelligence, lower self and higher self (as conceived by Assagioli and Jung). It has multiple centres of healing intelligence as well as the central ordering archetype of the Self.

Complex A knot of emotional suffering and buried memories caused by emotional injury, acting autonomously, located in the personal unconscious, and accessible to the early stages of psychotherapeutic investigation. Complexes connect to the deeper archetypal realm and to healing intelligence. Whitmont (1978) explains Jung's use of the word "complex" to cover, first, an outer shell, shaped by childhood traumas, personal events and conditioning, with a degree of autonomous functioning and not subject to the control of the ego; second, a mythological core, a universal human pattern with archetypal components. A close examination, therefore, of an individual's complexes leads to the deep psyche.

Coniunctio oppositorum Union of opposites, with particular reference to consciousness and the unconscious.

Countertransference Feelings and reactions of the psychotherapist concerning the client's projections, behaviour, feelings, and inner world.

Deep psyche A parallel term to the unconscious and referring to its two components: the personal unconscious and the collective unconscious. It derives from the term depth psychotherapy, originally coined by Eugen Bleuler, referring to all those psychotherapies that work with the unconscious; in these pages used to differentiate from the unconscious as conceived by Freud (a repressed id characterised by sexual and aggressive drives) and from an over-narrow Jungian-based definition, with the unconscious consisting mainly of archetypes.

Defences Unconscious defences against pain or threat. Primary defences threaten the embryonic self in early infancy before the emergence of a coherent ego. Secondary defences emerge later, after the formation of the ego, and are triggered when there are threats to it.

Depth psychotherapy Psychotherapy which acknowledges and works with the unconscious.

Ego It can be thought of in two ways: first, as a function of mind, providing a sense of planning, control, focus, and concentration; second, as the person one believes oneself to be, the centre of the subjective sense of identity, the experiential sense of coherence that is the centre of personality. Jung acutely described it as the subject of consciousness.

Ego consciousness A wide system of awareness at the centre of which are the concentrated control functions of the ego.

Enantiodrama A turning into the opposite; for example, that which was repressed may become conscious, that which was neglected may become dominant. It implies that the opposite lies within the subject.

Entelechy The process of becoming what one is meant to be; an unfolding of self; the intentionality and purposive drive of psychological growth.

Experiential Focusing A body-centered, experiential sensing method developed by Gendlin. Clients select a symptom or issue and focus on the bodily "feel" of it. These issues or symptoms are expressed emotionally and in language that resonates with the true feeling—"the bodily felt sense". This may be accompanied by images or symbols that can produce a "felt shift", producing a cathartic release and new meaning.

Healing intelligence The natural capacity of the psyche as a whole, also of its individual parts, to engage in self repair and integration, thus allowing growth and development to occur.

Hierosgamos The sacred marriage, for example, symbolically, between consciousness and the unconscious.

Hypnogogic States between sleep and wakefulness; light trance states.

Imaginal body The body viewed in a supra-sensory, imaginative manner; a form of spiritual or symbolic consciousness; sometimes called the subtle body. With respect to psychotherapy it can refer to body centres, like chakras, that are maps of the unconscious. Working with the complexes of the personal unconscious one contacts the energy of the deep psyche. The term does not mean imaginary or unreal.

Individuation Conceived by Jung as a four-stage development process in which first the shadow, second, the anima or animus, third, the archetypal spirit, and fourth, the Self are brought to consciousness; a process of becoming a more whole individual. It implies a release from the persona and over-identification with collective values and expectations. There is a continuous dialogue between ego and Self in which the centre of gravity of the personality moves from being initially centred at the pole of the ego to a mid-way position. Individuation, cautiously conceived, is not so much an end in itself as a process, a spiral around the Self, sometimes getting closer, sometimes moving away, but developing. In the first half of life individuation takes the form of adaptation to culture, the development of personality, talents, creativity, the creation of friendships, adaptations to intimacy, and possible reproduction; in the second half, consciousness may turn not to the outer but to the inner world and its archetypal foundation. Individuation is the natural development toward psychological growth and wholeness.

Inner awareness A special portion of consciousness able to look inwards in a non-analytic, open way, uncluttered by regret, aspiration, or duty; a meditative-type skill, distinct from analytic self-reflection, it can access material from the deep psyche, facilitate its integration; it also possesses great healing power. This is not ordinary self-reflection but a special introspective function, a pure awareness of one's inner world. Its activation requires that other parts of consciousness, especially those of a judging, assessing, filtering, and analysing nature, are temporarily switched off.

Integration The extent to which first, consciousness unites with parts of the deep psyche, and second, different parts of the deep psyche link with each other. Since the drive for such integration comes from outside of ego consciousness and can be seen in dreams and visualizations to derive from the deep psyche, then it indicates an archetype of order and growth, pushing for realisation, occurring when consciousness recognises, accepts, and integrates this entelechy.

Inter-subjective field In later stages of intensive psychotherapy the therapist may, at certain times, attune to the inner state of the client in a way that is beyond normal emotional and intuitive resonance. These experiences can be understood as the psyche of the client being a "shared field" with the therapist, and go beyond transference and countertransference reactions.

Jungian psychotherapist Practitioner working with the symbolic and archetypal nature of the unconscious. Some Jungians prefer to call themselves "analytical psychologists" but both these words are misleading since the emphasis of the deeper work is neither analytical nor psychological in the modern sense. The general term psychotherapist is often used in these pages.

Opus The work of transformation in the psyche.

Persona A mask or image of oneself presented to the external world—for example, a professional image.

Personal unconscious The first layer of the psyche contacted by consciousness as it engages in self exploration, typically containing personal character traits, personal history, early attachment relationships, complexes, and traumas. Psychotherapy, especially in the early stages, works on these areas intensively. When engaged with properly these naturally lead to the deeper psyche.

Potency The vitality of healing intelligence which has dynamic character features including expressiveness and receptivity.

Psyche The totality of consciousness and the unconscious often split into three parts: ego, personal unconscious, and the unconscious. The centre of consciousness is the ego; basic components of the personal unconscious include complexes; the collective unconscious is the emotional, instinctual, and spiritual foundation.

Psychoanalyst Psychotherapist with a Freudian training.

Psychotherapy A term here used very widely to cover psychoanalysis, psychotherapy, and counselling of many descriptions. The term depth psychotherapy is more precise since it refers to those therapies that work with the unconscious. However, since all readers are aware of the term "psychotherapy" I use this. Occasionally in this book the term "therapy" is used instead. It is characterised as a four-part process leading to integration and healing: 1) the establishment of a container and preliminary understanding of the symptoms, 2) the analysis of character, 3) the alignment to the deep psyche, 4) the integration process.

Scan The use of inner awareness to search the inner world and body centres where emotion and pain are stored so that healing can occur; requiring the suspension of ego consciousness.

Self Referring to the archetype of the Self and in Jungian psychology conceived of in two ways: first, as the totality of the psyche, conscious and unconscious; second, as the central archetype of order, an internal guidance system, orchestrating the development of personality. It is in the second sense that this concept is used in this book.

Shadow Parts of the personality not accepted by consciousness; often mixed with shame or guilt, they are easily projected on to others. They compensate for ego ideals and higher parts of personality. This concept is of great value not only in personal psychology but also for understanding mass movements and radical, political, group behaviours.

Spiritual Here referring to psychotherapy at an archetypal or foundational level—where the deepest human emotions touch the numinous and transcendent; also including the higher self and healing intelligence.

Synthetic As opposed to analytic understanding, this approach gathers meaning by bringing different parts together. Appreciating that material from the deep psyche is over-determined, symbolic, and condensed, this style uses a more intuitive approach.

Telos The goal or purpose of psychological growth.

Transcendent function Jung's term for a midway position between the ego and the Self, essential for the individuation process.

Transcendental love A universal love originating from a source outside of the ego, as if coming from above; psychologically, a higher source in the psyche.

Transference Feelings of a primary type, such as those originally experienced with parents, projected onto another; of specific concern in intensive psychotherapy where they are projected onto the psychotherapist.

Transpersonal A term used by Jung and signifying the numinous, collective unconscious beyond the personal psyche with its complexes, traumas, neuroses, and personal history.

Typology Jung's original contribution to a descriptive classification of personality in which four functions are outlined: thinking, feeling, sensation, and intuition; while two major axes (orientations) are indicated: introversion versus extroversion and judgement versus perception. Typically one of the functions allied with one of each of the positions on the axes are the dominants,—and lead character formation.

Unconscious The greater part of the psyche outside of consciousness consisting of the personal unconscious (buried memories, defence mechanisms, complexes) and the collective unconscious (archetypal world bordering on instincts and the foundation of healing intelligence); in these pages frequently referred to as deep psyche.

Visualizations As opposed to visions which may occur involuntarily, visualizations, as used in this book, refer to a specific stage within the scan when subjects seek images or a voice, like a dream, that elaborate the material of their suffering and can result in inspirational revelation.

REFERENCES

Assagioli, R. (1965). *Psychosynthesis*. New York: The Viking Press.

Balint, M. (1968). *The Basic Fault: Therapeutic Aspects of Regression*. London: Tavistock.

Chopra, D. (1989). *Quantum Healing: Exploring the Frontiers of Mind/Body Medicine*. London: Bantam.

Edinger, E. (1972). *Ego and Archetype*. New York: Penguin.

Erikson, E. H. (1950). *Childhood and Society*. New York: Norton.

Field, N. (1996). *Breakdown and Breakthrough*. London: Routledge.

Fordham, M. (1957). *New Developments in Analytical Psychology*. London: Routledge & Kegan Paul.

Fordham, M. (1960). Countertransference. In: Fordham, M., Gordon, R., Hubback, R. & Lambert, K. (Eds). *Techniques in Jungian Analysis*. London: Heinemann, 1974.

Freud, A. (1937). *The Ego and the Mechanisms of Defence*. London: Hogarth Press & Institute of Psycho-Analysis.

Garcia, A. (2010). *Humans Took Care of the Disabled Over 500,000 Years Ago*. Proceedings of the National Academy of Sciences. March 2010. Reported in http://discovermagazine.com/2010/jan-feb/082. Accessed 21 February 2011.

Gendlin, E. T. (1981). *Focusing*. New York: Bantam Books.

Goleman, D. (2005). *Emotional Intelligence*. New York: Bantam Books.

Grof, S. (1988). *The Adventure of Self-discovery*. Albany: SUNY Press.

Haines, S. & Sumner, G. (2010). *Cranial Intelligence: A Practical Guide to Biodynamic Craniosacral Therapy*. London: Singing Dragon.

Hillman, J. (1975). *Revisioning Psychology*. New York: HarperCollins.

Jacobi, M. (1990). *Individuation and Narcissism: the Psychology of Self in Jung and Kohut*. London: Routledge.

Johnson, S. C., Baxter, L. C., Wilder, L. S., Pipe, J. G., Heiserman, J. E. & Prigatano, G. P. (2002). Neural correlates of self-reflection. *Brain: A Journal of Neurology, 125*, 1808–1814.

Jonas, H. (1958). *The Gnostic Religion*. Boston: Beacon Press.

Jung, C. G. References are to the *Collected Works* (*CW*), by volume, paragraph and occasionally page number. Routledge & Kegan Paul, 1966, except as below.

Jung, C. G. (2009). Shamdasani, S. (Ed). *The Red Book: Liber Novus*. New York: W. W. Norton.

Jung, E. & von Franz, M. L. (1998). Translation Andrea Dykes, Second Edition. *The Grail Legend*. Princeton University Press.

Kalsched, D. (1996). *The Inner World of Trauma*. London: Routledge.

Kohut, H. (1971). *The Analysis of the Self*. New York: International Universities Press.

Leakey, R. (1992). *Origins Reconsidered*. London: Little, Brown and Company.

Mahrer, A. R. (1996). *The Complete Guide to Experiential Psychotherapy*. New York: John Wiley.

Neumann, E. (1988). *The Child: Structure and Dynamics of the Nascent Personality*. London: Karnac.

Rowan, J. (1993). *The Transpersonal: Spirituality in Psychotherapy and Counselling*. Second Edition. London: Routledge.

Samuels, A. (1989). *The Plural Psyche: Personality, Morality and the Father*. London: Routledge.

Schwartz-Salant, N. (1989). *The Borderline Personality: Vision and Healing*. Wilmette: Chiron.

Schwartz-Salant, N. (1998). *The Mystery of Human Relationship: Alchemy and the Transformation of Self*. London: Routledge.

Schwartz-Salant, N. & Stein, M. (Eds.) (1984). *Transference, Countertransference*. Wilmette: Chiron.

Sills, F. (2001). *Craniosacral Biodynamics: 1*. Berkeley, CA: North Atlantic Books.

Sollod, R. N. (1993). *Comprehensive Handbook of Psychotherapy and Integration*. New York: Plenum Press.

Spikins, P. A., Rutherford, H. E. & Needham, A. P. (2010). From Homininity to Humanity: Compassion from the Earliest Archaics to Modern Humans. *Time and Mind, 3*(3): 303–325.

Stein, M. (2005). Individuation: inner work. *Journal of Jungian Theory and Practice, 7*(2): 1–13.

Sterling, M. M. & Bugental, J. E. T. (1993). The meld experience in psychotherapy supervision. *Journal of Humanistic Psychology, 33*(2): 38–48.

Stolorow, R. D., Atwood, G. E. & Orange, D. M. (2002). *Worlds of Experience: Interweaving Philosophical and Clinical Dimensions in Psychoanalysis.* New York: Basic Books.

Symington, J. & Symington, N. (1996). *The Clinical Thinking of Wilfred Bion.* London: Routledge.

Taylor, R. P. (1985). *The Death and Resurrection Show.* London: Anthony Blond.

van Deurzen, E. (2002). *Existential Counselling and Psychotherapy in Practice.* London: Sage.

Vaughan, F. (1986). *The Inward Arc.* Boston & London: Shambhala.

Walker, A., Zimmerman, M. R. & Leakey R. E. F. (1982). A possible case of hypervitaminosis A in Homo Erectus. *Nature, 296*: 248–250.

Washburn, M. (1994). *Transpersonal Psychology in Psychoanalytic Perspective.* Albany: State University of New York Press.

Washburn, M. (1995). *The Ego and the Dynamic Ground.* Albany: State University of New York Press.

Welwood, J. (Ed) (1983). *Awakening the Heart: East/West Approaches to Psychotherapy and the Healing Relationship.* Boston & London: Shambhala.

Welwood, J. (2006). *Perfect Love, Imperfect Relationship.* Boston & London: Trumpeter.

Whitmont, E. C. (1993). *The Alchemy of Healing: Psyche and Soma.* Berkeley, CA. North Atlantic Books.

Winnicott, D. W. (1967). Mirror-role of mother and family in child development. In *Playing and Reality* (pp. 111–118). London: Tavistock.

Wordsworth, W. (1888). *The Complete Poetical Works of William Wordsworth.* London: MacMillan.

INDEX